Merri my love!
What would we have been
without this place? I'll really
miss your help finding the
perfect eggplant.
Thank you so much for
your non-stop action-packed
love & friendship — you
are super marvelous!
I'll meet you in
the mountains!

♡
Lauren

Kensington

Kensington

Jean Cochrane

with photographs by Vincenzo Pietropaolo

The BOSTON MILLS PRESS

Cataloging in Publication Data

Cochrane, Jean, 1932–
   Kensington

ISBN 1-55046-338-1

1. Kensington Market (Toronto, Ont.) — History —
Pictorial works. 2. Kensington (Toronto, Ont.) — History —
Pictorial works. 3. Minorities — Ontario — Toronto — History —
Pictorial works. 4. Toronto (Ont.) — History — Pictorial works.
I. Title.

FC3097.52.C62 2000   971.3'541   C00-931858-5
F1059.5.T686K46 2000

Published in 2000 by
Boston Mills Press
132 Main Street
Erin, Ontario N0B 1T0
Tel 519-833-2407
Fax 519-833-2195
e-mail books@bostonmillspress.com
www.bostonmillspress.com

An affiliate of
Stoddart Publishing Co. Limited
34 Lesmill Road
Toronto, Ontario, Canada
M3B 2T6
Tel 416-445-3333
Fax 416-445-5967
e-mail gdsinc@genpub.com

Distributed in Canada by
General Distribution Services Limited
325 Humber College Boulevard
Toronto, Canada M9W 7C3
Orders 1-800-387-0141 Ontario & Quebec
Orders 1-800-387-0172 NW Ontario & other provinces
e-mail cservice@genpub.com

Distributed in the United States by
General Distribution Services Inc.
PMB 128, 4500 Witmer Industrial Estates,
Niagara Falls, New York 14305-1386
Toll-free 1-800-805-1083
Toll-free fax 1-800-481-6207
e-mail gdsinc@genpub.com
www.genpub.com

Sponsored by
St. Stephen's Community House
91 Bellevue Avenue
Toronto, Ontario, Canada
M5T 2N8
Tel 416-925-2103
Fax 416-925-2271
www.ststephenshouse.com

Design by Mary Firth
Photo research by Jean Cochrane

Printed in Canada

THE CANADA COUNCIL | LE CONSEIL DES ARTS
FOR THE ARTS | DU CANADA
SINCE 1957 | DEPUIS 1957

We acknowledge for their financial support of our publishing program the Canada
Council, the Ontario Arts Council, and the Government of Canada through the
Book Publishing Industry Development Program (BPIDP).

Contents

PREFACE

When I think of Kensington, words like tolerant, diverse, colourful and funky come to mind. It is a world unto itself, a self-contained community, surrounded by low-rise apartment buildings, old houses, and lately, newly developed condomini-ums. It has community centres, churches and synagogues, schools, banks, social services, alterna-tive stores, restaurants and cafes, a hospital, fire hall, library, university and several tiny parkettes. The area is boxed by the Alexandra Park public housing development and Chinatown on the south and east, and by trendy College Street and the prosperous homes of the Annex on the north and west. Kensington itself has just about everything, all mixed up together, in just a few short blocks.

It is one of the most dynamic neighbourhoods in Toronto.

The story of how Kensington came about is no less fascinating than its life today. Kensington was created as wave after wave of immigrants made it their first home in Toronto. Many stayed. Today there are signs everywhere of their continuing presence, giving Kensington a multi-cultural dimension that is unparalleled.

In 1974, St. Stephen's Community House became independent of the Anglican Church, incorporating as a nonprofit charitable organiza-tion. The work, without the religious affiliation, continued more or less unchanged. As we approached our 25th anniversary and the new millennium simultaneously, it seemed fitting to mark the occasion with something special, some-thing to last. St. Stephen's had twice produced small booklets—one called *Kensington Roots* and the other, *The Story of St. Stephen's Community House, 1962 to 1984*. However, no comprehensive book on the history of Kensington had ever been written. In fact, Spadina Avenue was as close as any-one got. And so the idea for this book was born.

My attachment to Kensington goes back to my high-school days, when my art class came downtown on a "field trip" to sketch Kensington. I remember thinking how completely different this place was. It smelled of fish and spices. People talked in languages I didn't understand. The side-walks were crowded and there was a perpetual traffic jam in its narrow streets, where trucks were unloading carcasses of cows and pigs. There were live chickens and pigeons being sold from cages on the streets. I was mesmerized.

Who would have guessed that I would end up living there, in one of those low-rise apartment buildings, and working at the local community centre? Although I no longer live there now, I continue to work in the heart of Kensington at St. Stephen's Community House, having never stopped feeling a deep attachment to this neighbourhood.

The hope is that this book will serve to enlighten people—both residents of Toronto and visitors to the city—about the evolution and rich cultural heritage of this wonderful place called Kensington. It is a must-see destination for visitors and one that Torontonians should regularly frequent if they wish to shop in a unique, open-air market for fresh local produce, coffees from around the world, cheeses galore or freshly baked Jamaican patties. Its restaurants offer tasty food from many countries, and there are great buys for fashion-seekers looking for funk or chic.

Mostly, however, we wish to celebrate Kensington's spirit. Among so many other things, it is also a community of people who are often passionately divided in their vision for the neighbourhood. But somehow, things do get done and Kensington continues to grow and change, while maintaining its character. This book is a celebration, an affirmation of how people from diverse cultures, religions, economic backgrounds and interests, can come together and, against all odds, create a uniquely tolerant community and a place that we can all call home.

Liane Regendanz
Executive Director
St. Stephen's Community House
June 2000

downtown Toronto. Programs reach out to and help the most vulnerable members of this inner-city neighbourhood — children and their families, disadvantaged youth, frail seniors, newcomers to Canada, people who are at risk of contracting AIDS, the unemployed and those who are homeless.

A member of the United Way of Greater Toronto, St. Stephen's Community House is supported by all three levels of government, foundations, corporations, churches, service clubs, individual donors, fundraising and productive enterprises. Over 400 volunteers complement the work of 265 paid staff who deliver programs out of eleven locations in the community.

St. Stephen's Employment & Training Centre
Creating Opportunities Strengthening Communities

STRENGTHENING COMMUNITIES
25
SINCE 1974

TF
TORONTO COMMUNITY FOUNDATION
FOR TORONTO. FOR GOOD.

TORONTO Millennium
2000 - 2001

Kensington
HEALTH CENTRE

United Way
of Greater Toronto

Leonard Avenue in 1908. — CITY OF TORONTO ARCHIVES, SC 244-2321

Chapter 1 How It Started

Kensington is an old part of the city. Its houses, many of them, were built in the 1870s and 1880s. The market that has given it a kind of fame is layered over with the struggles and hopes of a richly varied succession of immigrant groups.

Its institutions—the church and the fire hall at the top of Bellevue; the synagogues deep in its heart; the park, cleared out of the forest and once a parade ground for a rich man's militia unit—all have seen changes that have matched and even foreshadowed changes in the life of Toronto.

Kensington has always had an interior life of its own. It has always been a home, a workplace, a village. Its people know its boundaries—Spadina to Bathurst, College to Dundas—and they know their neighbours. They have found it both a refuge and a place to work their way out of. They have fought hard to maintain it, and it has left its mark on everyone who ever lived there.

The Denisons were an unlikely family to be the European founders of Kensington. Nineteenth-century, high Tory, Anglican military landowners, they were a complex, colourful, belligerent and partisan extended family who owned large tracts of downtown Toronto west of Spadina and sold them to make a profit and a city.

The earliest Canadian Denison was Captain John, who came from Yorkshire as a friend of Peter Russell, which was a good thing to be in the infant town of York. Russell was a power—in 1796 he was administrator of what is now Ontario, and he looked after John. Russell's half-sister Elizabeth even gave John's wife Sophia a slave as a Christmas present. (It is said that Sophia freed her.)

The Denisons' Belle Vue home as it looked in 1865. — ARCHIVES OF ONTARIO, 1582 S1305

Captain John briefly managed Russell's farm, Petersfield, which stretched from Queen Street to Bloor Street just east of Spadina. It was one of a series of thirty park lots that sliced up the densely wooded land between the Don River and Landsdowne. When Lieutenant Governor John Graves Simcoe decided to move Upper Canada's capital from Niagara to Toronto in 1793, he used some of the park lots to lure friends of the government to the newer, rawer town, apparently with the vision of a society made up of a landed upper class.

The British had taken possession of the land as part of a massive land sale treaty signed first in 1787 in Prince Edward County with three Mississauga Native chiefs. The treaty covered an area between Lake Simcoe and the north shore of Lake Ontario. The southern part of the Toronto segment covered the lakeshore from roughly the Etobicoke River to the Scarborough Bluffs.

Denison soon bought his own park lots along what is now Ossington, as well as a farm, Black Creek, in the Weston area. When he died in 1824 he left most of his estate to the eldest of his sons, George Taylor Denison I, and it was this first George who was the Kensington Denison.

George Denison inherited more land and useful United Empire Loyalist connections from his first father-in-law, Richard Lippincott. He would marry four times, doing well in each case, and

would outlive three of his wives and six of his thirteen children. By the time he died in 1853, his will was reported to be the largest ever probated in Upper Canada, his wealth estimated at £200,000, including title to 556 Toronto acres.

It was in 1815 that he bought park lot 17 and half of 18, the land between Major and Lippincott Streets, which then had Russell Creek running through it. At its core was most of Kensington.

When he bought the lots near Peter Russell's farm they were well to the west of the town, which then had about 1,500 people, a few government and business buildings and a hundred or so houses in its downtown area around Yonge and Front Streets.

In his lifetime and his son's, a period of less than one hundred years, Denison's forest and farm would become a thriving neighbourhood in a bustling Victorian city. He built his home, Belle Vue, more or less in the middle of his property. In his description of the property, Toronto's early chronicler, Henry Scadding, noted, "This thoroughfare [Denison Avenue] was in the first instance the drive up to the homestead of the estate, Belle Vue, a large, white, cheery-looking abode lying far back but pleasantly visible from Lot Street [Queen] through a long vista of overhanging trees. From the old Belle Vue have spread populous colonies at Dovercourt, Rusholme and

Lieutenant Colonel Robert
B. Denison, Deputy Adjutant
General of the Canadian Militia.

— *MACLEAN'S MAGAZINE,* CHRISTMAS
1913

In 1869 the Denison home, in
the centre of what is now
Kensington, was surrounded by
orchards and watered by Russell
Creek, but around their oasis,
building lots were swiftly
filling in.

— TORONTO REFERENCE LIBRARY

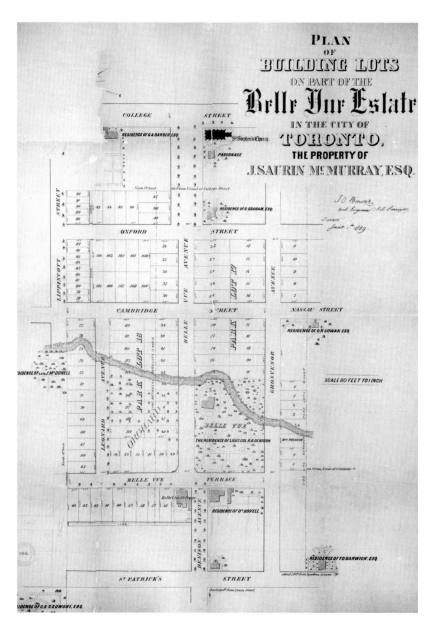

elsewhere, marked, like their progenitor, with vigour of character and evincing in a succession of instances strong aptitude for military affairs."

It was George Denison's sons who formed the populous colonies on estates to the west, between Dufferin and Ossington Streets. One of his grandsons wrote a family memoir that evokes an atmosphere hard to imagine now, describing his walks across the fields from Belle Vue to visit his uncle, George II, at Dovercourt and College.

Providing a flavour of the family and a picture of the days when Toronto could go sleighing on its frozen waterfront, he describes Uncle George as "an expert skater, and my father [who was Robert] relates that they used to be annoyed when driving on the Bay, by toughs snow-balling them, and then skating safely away. One day his brother fastened on his skates and hid a heavy black snake whip in the sleigh. The snow-balling began, when out jumped Uncle George, and created consternation among the boys, as the fleetest of them were unable to escape the heavy whip, which the unexpected skater plied with much vigor."

Neighbours during the time the Denisons owned Belle Vue included the MacDonells, who farmed at Bathurst and Dundas where Toronto Western Hospital now sprawls; the Gzowskis, in what is now Alexandra Park; and the Boultons, at the Grange at Dundas and McCaul, where the Art Gallery of Ontario now stands; and government house, at King and Simcoe on the site of present-day Roy Thompson Hall.

The lives of the Denisons were the lives of prosperous, conservative gentry, which included business and public duties, church and military service. But the Denisons were, above all, military.

In 1834, York, with 9,254 citizens, was incorporated and called Toronto again. In its first election, George Denison and Dr. John Rolph were elected aldermen for St. Patrick's Ward. Rolph would go on to join the new mayor, William Lyon Mackenzie, in rebellion in 1837.

It was a short-lived and short-tempered council, with Denison decidedly one of those on the other side. In 1830 when Mackenzie was editor of the *Colonial Advocate,* Denison had offered publicly to give him "a slap in the chops." So when the uprising started, the militia unit known as Denison's Horse was called in on active duty. Denison had raised the unit in 1822, and it was to be the forerunner of the present Governor General's Horse Guard. Referred to as the nursery of Toronto's militia, its first eight commanding officers were Denisons.

Kensington must have bristled with martial splendour at times, for Bellevue Square, in front of the family home, was an occasional parade ground, and the fields at College and Bellevue were the

scene of militia musters. In 1913 *Maclean's Magazine* did a story entitled, "The Fighting Denisons." The article, which began with John and covered the generations down to his great grandsons, counted three colonels, five lieutenant colonels, one major, two captains and an admiral.

In the meantime George Denison was selling his land, filling in the streets to the south of Belle Vue. He was planning to sell more lots to the north when he died in 1853. Robert, who was his third son, inherited Belle Vue, and would subdivide and sell what remained of the old estate. When he died in 1900 he was no longer a landowner, and the Kensington area was built up almost solidly from College to Dundas.

Robert Denison took his turn as councilman for St. Patrick's during the 1840s. He had begun his military career in 1843, and was deputy adjutant general of Military District No. 2 when he retired in 1886. He also shared the family talent for publicized public disputes.

The architect of St. Stephen's painted this watercolour of the proposed church. Thomas Fuller designed the Parliament buildings in Ottawa and the University Avenue Armoury in Toronto. The inscription reads: "N.E. view of the church at S. Stephen. Toronto Canada West. To Robert Brittain Denison Esq. Of Toronto. This view dedicated by his faithful servant, the architect."

St. Stephen's and its rectory burned in October 1865. Sunday services were held at University College until the church was rebuilt and opened in March 1866. The architect this time was Henry Langley, who worked on the Metropolitan Church, St. James Cathedral and McMaster College, now the Royal Conservatory of Music.

— COURTESY ST. STEPHEN'S-IN-THE-FIELD

It was Robert Denison who created the family's lasting legacy to Kensington, by donating land at Bellevue and College and building the Anglican Church of St. Stephen the Proto-Martyr, known familiarly as St. Stephen's-in-the-Field. A church history describes the original setting that gave rise to the name: "On July 1, 1858, a cloudy, chilly day, the corner-stone of St. Stephen's Church was laid by John Strachan the first Anglican Bishop of Toronto in the middle of a large field. College Street had not then been built—there were only two houses near—one on Bellevue south of our present buildings and one on College Street west of Bellevue Avenue."

Two years after the church opened its doors, its generous benefactor created an uproar over a doctrinal dispute with its first minister, the Rev. J. H. McCollum. It was carried on in high Victorian tones, and in letters published in the *Globe,* and distributed to the no-doubt fascinated congregation. On December 18, 1860, McCollum wrote, "I have felt this long time that my preaching, the naked and simple gospel of Jesus Christ—although acceptable to the ninety-nine hundredths of the congregation, was not acceptable to all, and finding that the minority ruled in the Church, I have been contemplating a change, and intended leaving a place where my hands were so tied and my usefulness so impaired."

Above and facing page: In 1911, No. 8 Hose Station across from the church at College and Bellevue became the first to get a motor-driven fire engine, which used both chemicals and water to fight fires. It was so successful that city council voted to buy more the following year, but also prudently bought a horse-drawn vehicle.

— COURTESY TORONTO FIRE DEPARTMENT

Below and facing page: The Anglican Sisterhood of St. John the Divine had been operating church homes for the aged since 1886, first on Larch Street, then on John. In 1907 they bought Dr. Temple's hospital on Bellevue. An addition, built as a home for the Pepler family, and known as Bellevue House, became the Gwenneth Osler Memorial Wing. The home accommodated about forty-five elderly women.

During those years they also managed the Hospital for the Treatment of Women on Euclid, then on Major. It was a forerunner of the Doctors Hospital.

Left: Dining room in home for aged, about 1910. Right: On voting day in 1958, one-hundred-year-old Mrs. Ford cast her ballot. With her are Mrs. Thompson, Sister Constance and Mrs. Carscadden.

— COURTESY SISTERHOOD OF ST. JOHN THE DIVINE

Left and facing page: Bell Canada's central office was built at Bellevue Avenue and Oxford Street in 1907. It was a telephone exchange and home to the Bell Telephone School for Operators. It was closed in 1932 because technological change made it redundant. Since 1954 it has been home to Precision Vacuum Products.

— BELL CANADA HISTORICAL SERVICES

Denison replied on December 24, "I can scarcely fancy you allude to me, as I have always endeavoured to increase your usefulness .. . in answer to your question with regard to last Sunday's sermon, why was it not objected to when preached months before? The reason is this, your sermons have often grieved me and my family immensely, but we bore with them until our patience was thoroughly exhausted, and then and not till then did I allude to them. . . .

"A change must take place within a short time, in St. Stephen's or my family and I must worship elsewhere."

Early in 1861 an Anglican church publication, the *Echo,* carried an editorial deploring the situation. The writer acknowledged that the church and parsonage were Denison's own property, but said indignantly, "One might almost suppose that Mr. Denison imagined himself to be lord paramount of the whole ecclesiastical establishment of St. Stephen's."

In April 1861 the Rev. J. H. McCollum left for St. Thomas, and about one hundred parishioners signed a letter wishing him well. The Rev. Canon Broughall, appointed by Bishop Strachan, would be rector at St. Stephen's for the next fifty years.

St. Stephen's was taken over formally by the Anglican Church and consecrated on Sunday, May 17, 1863. But the memory must have lingered on, for Robert Denison's son wrote, "During the Fenian excitement of 1866, the guard at the armouries was inspected at 8 P.M., and I can hear yet the clank of my father's spurs leaving the North door before the sermon. Unkind people used to say, 'Colonel Denison left the church before the sermon because he disapproved of the Incumbent's doctrine.'"

St. Stephen's soon had one of the largest congregations in Toronto, the city of churches. It stood at 600, plus a Sunday School of 650. In 1862, Denison had donated more land, and a school was built beside the church, in those days before the public school system was operating fully. It would have a long life as part of a group of church buildings that included a gym, where the boys and young men of the Bible class boxed and did their calisthenics and, in 1891, organized a hare-and-hounds chase for Thanksgiving day.

In that year, thirty years after the dedication, a contemporary description of College and Bellevue was that it was "entirely built on and densely peopled." Toronto's building blocks were being put into place. There were 86,415 people in the city, more than 80,000 of whom were of English, Irish

or Scottish origin, and its outlook reflected that. The 1880 census counted 932 industries in the city; there was a stock exchange, Consumer's Gas, and the Dominion Telegraph Company. The Canadian National Exhibition had begun in 1879, and Eaton's had opened in 1869 at Queen and Yonge. There were prosperous merchants, banks, wholesale warehouses, and small factories lining King and Front and Wellington. The railroads and the heavier industries were moving west along the lakeshore. For a while Kensington fit right in, with its respectable homes and its own building blocks.

The Richards family owned a store at Nassau and Lippincott. Kensington's nonconforming mix of business and living quarters on interior streets, away from main avenues, began even before the Jewish market took shape a few blocks away. Above: Mr. and Mrs. Richards with Alice and Nellie about 1914.

— ONTARIO JEWISH ARCHIVES, 2945

Left: Alice and Nellie Richards, 1904. This is probably Nassau Street.

— ONTARIO JEWISH ARCHIVES, 2946

Facing page: In 1905, Mrs. Richards was selling Quaker Oats and Aunt Sally's pancake flour, and promoting candidate Hacker for city council.

— ONTARIO JEWISH ARCHIVES, 2944

P.197 Oct. 14. 1913 BELLEVUE SQUARE

Bellevue Square as it looked in 1913.   — CITY OF TORONTO ARCHIVES, RG 8-52-197

Across from St. Stephen's was a fire hall, built in 1878. People enjoyed coming out to stroll and to watch the fire horses being exercised. Then, in 1911, No. 8 Fire Station became one of the first in Toronto to have a motorized fire engine. Another touch of the modern was at Oxford and Bellevue, where in 1907 Bell Telephone built offices to house an exchange and a school for operators.

At St. Stephen's, Georgina Broughall, the rector's wife, was one of the founders of the Anglican Sisterhood of St. John the Divine, which opened a hospital on Major Street that would become the Doctors Hospital. In 1906 the order also took over a private hospital on Bellevue and established the Church Home for the Aged, which survived there until 1978. Sir William Osler was one of its early supporters, donating an addition on Oxford Street.

That started the east side of Bellevue on its history as welfare row.

Broughall's daughter was married to Dr. Henry Machell, who ran his medical practice from 95 Bellevue Avenue until 1914. Their house would become a Salvation Army refuge for women, and begin its work as a day-care centre during the Second World War. Number 91, home to the minister of College Street Presbyterian Church during the 1890s, would become St. Stephen's Community House.

Lansdowne School opened on Spadina Circle in 1888. To the south, the original Ryerson School near Dundas and Bathurst was built in 1876. Toronto Western Hospital took over the MacDonell farmhouse in 1899 and would put up a hospital building in 1905. In the middle of Kensington, Robert Denison had offered largish lots for sale in the 1870s for $350 each, but they didn't move, so he divided them again in three. The result was a sprinkling of small houses that filled with English immigrants.

The city directory of 1880 shows a William D'Arcy on Nassau Street; he was a clerk of the pension office. His neighbours included Messrs. Curry, a telephone operator; Murdoc, an insurance agent; and John Palmer, a peddler; plus a carpenter and a printer.

In 1900 many of the houses on Augusta were owned by landlords, which would be the case in Kensington for decades. Their tenants included a policeman, a shoemaker, a labourer, a gardener, an electrician, a waiter and another printer.

Robert Denison sold Belle Vue in 1889. It was demolished shortly afterwards, and two houses were built in its place. But the Denisons left their stamp in many ways, such as in area street names Denison, Bellevue, Major, Robert, Borden and Lippincott, which are all connected to the family. They also donated the old parade ground to the city in 1897. Denison Square is now Bellevue Square, a well-used park. With that and the involvement of St. Stephen's Church in the community, the ghosts of the Denisons may still be said to anchor Kensington.

Arriving at Union Station in Toronto in 1910. — PRINGLE AND BOOTH, NATIONAL ARCHIVES OF CANADA, C-047042

CHAPTER 2 THE WARD

Then there was the Ward, where Kensington's first Jews probably came from. The Ward, nicknamed for St. John's Ward, was across University Avenue. It was the next ward east of St. Patrick's. It was a slum that sprawled untidily from just below College to Bay and down to Queen.

Toronto had long had a minuscule Jewish population, fewer than 200 in the mid-nineteenth century, mostly from England, and largely middle class. One or two even lived on Jarvis Street with the rest of the Establishment. But the new wave had begun by 1900. There were 3,000 Jews in the city at that time, and by 1913 there would be 32,000, in a total city population that had ballooned past 200,000. These new Jews were considered outlandish, with their beards, odd hats and unfamiliar languages. They scratched out a living as peddlers, as dealers in junk and secondhand clothes, operating tiny stores in the Ward or working in the sweatshops of the needle trades.

Most of them were from the rural villages of Eastern Europe and Russia, driven out by persecution. Most of them were Orthodox. They chose these ways of making a living because that was what was available to them, partly because their skills had been limited by restrictions in their home countries on the trades they could enter. As well, the peddlers and storekeepers were self-employed, and thus free to observe the Sabbath properly, home by Friday evening with no one insisting they be at work on Saturday.

St. Stephen's-in-the-Field in 1911, shot by Toronto photographer William James. — CITY OF TORONTO ARCHIVES, SC 244-7250

They were not the only people living in the Ward. There were Italian immigrants digging the new sewer systems and streetcar lines, and there were Blacks, most of whom worked for the railroads nearby. Although some of their families had been in Canada for generations, they were not welcome elsewhere. The poor Irish were relegated to the sneeringly named Cabbagetown.

But it was the Jews who seemed to draw the heaviest scorn from Toronto's Anglo citizenry. In *The Canadian Magazine* of July 1913 there was an article called "The Melting Pot," by Margaret Bell, and it read,

> You are now among the Jewish inhabitants of The Ward. . . . An old man stands on a little bit of ground between a shop and the sidewalk, fanning a charcoal fire in a large tin boiler. He has great woolly whiskers and wears a shirt of red flannel. He might be an ancient prophet, casting a spell over his enemies.
>
> But he is only a tinker, mending brass and copper kettles.
>
> You speak to him. A cunning look creeps into his eyes, and he regards you from under quizzical eyebrows. He does not trust any respectably dressed person who happens to saunter through that part of town. For he did not receive a licence slip from the City Hall that year.

> When you ask him how much he charges for mending a copper kettle, he pretends he is deaf, and you may shout until all the ragamuffins of the street ridicule you into silence.
>
> Innumerable tumbledown shacks stand in a state of slatternly decay, on both sides of the street. . . .

The Jews built a community structure in the midst of poverty and rejection: synagogues, Jewish schools, English classes, a medical dispensary, and stores and tearooms that were gathering places for news and discussion, discussion that may sometimes have centred on the missionaries in their midst. Religion was a powerful force in Canadian society at the turn of the last century, and there was a muscular, evangelizing Christianity at work. The churches, sending their missionaries out into the world, did not forget their own backyards.

There were several missions to the Jews set up in the Ward, including the Anglican Nathanael Institute, opened in 1912. The Presbyterian Church was sending in missionaries, some of whom were converted Jews who could speak Yiddish, to preach on street corners. They were resented. A 1911 newspaper report said, "Eight arrests were made as the result of a riot at Agnes and Elizabeth Streets last night among an assemblage of the Jewish population who rose in arms against the presence on the corner of a Christian

A restaurant on Agnes Street, now Dundas. The picture appeared in the *Toronto World* in December 1910, headed, "Picturesque if not Artistic, Glimpses of the Ward." — CITY OF TORONTO ARCHIVES, SC 244-291

An article by Margaret Bell on the Ward appeared in *The Canadian Magazine* in 1913. It described life there in unsympathetic terms. "Inside one of the doors, you catch a glimpse of a little girl rocking a sick baby. The room is tiny, but it contains a cook stove, a table, two or three chairs and an equal number of beds. Beds undoubtedly, but from all appearances, piles of filthy rags thrown in indiscriminate piles on the floor. What should be another living room is a miniature grocery shop where one may buy ice cream from dirty cones, or cakes which hang in the window, on a bit of greasy brown paper."

worker, who they claim was sent there for the express purpose of attacking their religion.

"As soon as they were brought to the police station, Jewish sympathizers swarmed the police desk, offering to give bonds for any amount required."

The end result appears to have been police protection for the missionaries.

The drift westward out of the Ward began, partly because from the 1890s on the area was being squeezed. There were proud new institutions displacing what one contemporary author called "old rookeries and dilapidated relics of a bygone day." The University of Toronto was long established at College, and the city hall had recently been built at Bay. The University Avenue Armoury had claimed a large chunk at Osgoode Street, and Toronto General Hospital ate up another eight acres in 1909. The 1904 fire that destroyed so much of the business area also had a long-range effect, because in its aftermath the clothing manufacturers would move west to lower Spadina.

The Ward was also a prime target for clean-up as the public health movement took hold. A 1910 report called for strong measures to rid the city of sewerless, crowded slums where illness and death bred in the overflowing privies and muddy alleyways. Its author, Medical Officer of Health Dr. Charles Hastings, condemned a policy that

According to Toronto Health Department reports on this scene from Agnes Street (now Dundas) in November 1913, "The filth and disorder pictured are not peculiar to this backyard. Similar conditions were seen in many properties in the Ward and in other localities throughout the city. It was learned that four months ago two children were removed, owing to scarlet fever, to the isolation hospital, and another child had just returned from the hospital, having had the same disease. In this yard, a very unsanitary toilet was found." — CITY OF TORONTO ARCHIVES, SC 244-291

brought immigrants to Canada and did not look after them. A 1918 municipal report castigated speculators who were holding properties in the Ward, doing nothing to improve it.

It is possible that the peddlers may have discovered Kensington and brought word back. This former domain of the Denisons had what would now be called affordable housing, and the move began.

A 1910 city directory shows five people with Jewish names living in tiny Kensington Place, all of them working for Eaton's as pressers, finishers, or operators. In 1911, Baldwin Street, which would soon see the beginnings of the Jewish Market, was still home to a grocery store operated by a man named Mclean. He shared this better address with Nathan Spector, a teacher, and Louis Gurofsky, who was in insurance, and who had run as alderman in 1909.

Kensington was a great improvement on the Ward. Interior streets were still roughly paved, but modern pavement was coming down Bathurst. There were streetcars on College and Spadina and sewers were going in along Bellevue. The pattern

Men like these gathered old clothes and rags from prosperous parts of town for secondhand resale or for shredding and use in factories such as paper makers. Note the Elm Street address, in the Ward. — NATIONAL ARCHIVES OF CANADA, PA 086456

Kensington's first Jewish merchants were surely the peddlers selling from carts and horse-drawn wagons, some of them rented. There were, of course, stables and blacksmith shops in the area.

the outskirts of the city. Brand new houses inhabited by well-to-do business and professional men were springing up around it, and the boys and girls who flocked to its portals when the bell rang from the quaint old cupola were all of British or Canadian parentage.

"Today Ryerson and the Ryerson neighborhood have succumbed to the Hebrew invasion. The school, which has developed into the biggest in Toronto in point of attendance (40 rooms, 1,800 children), is filled to the extent of seventy-five percent by Hebrew children.

"All the former Ryerson traditions have gone by the board, and between the days when Samuel McAllister, the school's first principal, stamped the impress of a fine character of an older generation and the present era, when a different race of people have thronged into the district, there is a distinct break. New traditions are now being evolved, which, let it be hoped, will exert as great an influence for good in the coming years."

The change accelerated when immigration started again after the First World War and would soon be complete. By 1931 there would be 45,305 Jews in Toronto, and 80 percent of them lived in Kensington and surrounding streets—Major, Brunswick, and Palmerston, and across Spadina on Beverley, Cecil, and McCaul. A new village had been born.

was beginning—old immigrants moved out, new ones moved in. This transformation was spelled out in a 1916 story in the *Toronto Star,* one of a series on historic schools. "It takes a visit to a school like Ryerson to drive home impressively the rapidly changing character of the older sections of Toronto. Ryerson (built in 1876) once stood near

CHAPTER 3   THE MARKET

If immigrants try to build a bit of home around themselves in the new country, the Jews of Kensington succeeded beyond most. Kensington and its adjacent streets became an almost self-sufficient village. The Yiddish word for it is *shtetl.*

The Market was the bread basket, a resource, a meeting place, a touch of home in an alien world. It was like an Eastern European market, with its crated chickens, live fish, pickles and cheeses made in the back room, and the smell of bagels and bread wafting over it all. You bargained, and if your English wasn't perfect, who noticed? You bought by the bushel, or you brought your own bottle and bought ten cents worth of oil. You could put it on the cuff, and you could have it delivered.

It began with a few people selling from rented pushcarts, wagons, spaces in front of houses and stores on Kensington and Baldwin. It was called the Jewish Market, and open mostly on Thursday and Friday, for shopping before the Sabbath. Far from being a tourist attraction, it was shunned by most of Toronto's citizenry. The neighbourhood it served during its heyday, in the '20s, '30s and '40s, was filled with immigrants—not only Jews, but Italians, Ukrainians, Hungarians, and a scattering of Blacks.

Sam Lunansky, whose mother started a fruit store in about 1930, says, "Everyone came to this area because I think it reminded them of their own villages, because it was like a secluded village. . . . Everybody seemed to be a part, it doesn't matter what nationality, everybody was at ease here. Some people were very rude, if you didn't speak the language properly out of this area, they let you know it. But if you came in here, it didn't matter what you spoke.

Photo taken by a St. Christopher House staff person, about 1916. Possibly on Wales Avenue. — COURTESY ST. CHRISTOPHER HOUSE

About 1914, this may be in the Ward. — NATIONAL ARCHIVES OF CANADA, PA-084968

Baldwin Street in 1922, now complete with motorized trucks.

— NATIONAL ARCHIVES OF CANADA, PA-084813

"It was very friendly and secure, I'll tell you that. Because there was a lot of discrimination at that time, if you were Jewish.

"The only time I got out of here I went to the air force, and I found myself kind of leery. I was only eighteen, and it was a little bit of a shock, because you lived in this environment like a bubble."

Max Katz's family started out on Chestnut Street, where the Hospital for Sick Children is now. "You went to all the stores and sampled food. Met all your friends there. Everybody came there to do their shopping once a week for Shabbot. Came there Thursday and bought their chickens there and they had them slaughtered there and had them plucked there. And everything there you needed, cheeses and herring and meat, fruit, all kinds of European foods.

"And you went to the bakery for one thing, and then you went to the fish store and you bought your sour pickles there."

His wife Sadie recalls, "Everything was out on the streets. We didn't go inside a store—everything was outside the store. And it was very, very busy, you had to just wait your turn or push your way in to get served. We walked up and down the streets looking who was the cheapest, who's got the best bargains. Two dollars had to last us."

The bargaining was sharp, and both shoppers and sellers kept shrewd eyes open to keep each other honest. The merchants competed loudly, hawking their bargains, the freshness of their fruit. "They were like barkers," says Lunansky. "People were more expressive than they are now—it was rowdy, it was very noisy."

Katz says, "In later years, during my mother's lifetime, my father would buy papers from the newspapers downtown and he would unfold them and roll them up into fifty-pound bales and sell them to the fish stores to wrap up their fish.

"My father always worked the night shift, and after he came home from work he'd grab a couple of hours sleep . . . then he would get somebody with a truck to go down and pick the papers up. . . . He had about ten or twelve customers he did that for. We made our delivery once a week, I suppose."

Kensington is built on that kind of tiny enterprise. Sam Lunansky says his mother, Sonia, started with a broken box and a scale, renting a space in front of a store on Augusta. "We sold on the outside. Rain, shine, it was always in the open." His father eventually quit his needle job and became the buyer, going to the wholesale fruit-and-vegetable market that was in the old Great Western railway station near Front and Yonge. Almost all of the Market's produce came from the farms that surrounded Toronto.

"He started to go out buying," says Lunansky, "and at that time the wholesale was down near the St. Lawrence Market, and maybe one of the farmers would bring the goods to this area, because we didn't have a vehicle. It started off small quantities with basically potatoes, onions, carrots, beets, cabbage. It was a seasonal business, and people bought in bulk because they had large families and they knew how to cook."

He says that in the winter, once they were able to rent the whole store at 249 Augusta: "We had a little stove going, the little coal stove. It was a different scene altogether than it is now. You had fishmongers—trucks used to come with big vats of live carp. People knew what to do with the carp, knew how to bake it. You could keep 30-pound carps, huge things off the trucks. You took the carp home, kept it alive in the bathtub until it was needed, then hit it on the head, cleaned it and baked it.

Joseph and Bayla Nesker came from Poland and ran their store on Baldwin Street from 1923 to about 1936. Son Harry helped with deliveries, towing his wagon to customers' homes.   — COURTESY HARRY NESKER

Kalmen Greenspan began selling kosher meat in Kensington about 1914. He expanded to Brunswick Avenue, into the wholesale trade, and out of the area. In 1939, he and his niece Sheila posed with his son Harry and wife Rebecca. Their Kensington phone number was Beverly 1833. — *COURTESY HARRY GREENSPAN*

"And they had chickens, live chickens right in front, ducks, different kinds of noises you wouldn't get now. And then you had so many variations of pickled food—you had herrings, barrels of herrings on the street, you know they were about four feet, big vats of herring, different kinds, and they had fish stores that had tanks of different kinds of fish, live fish. And pickled watermelon. Kaplan's cheese store used to make the best cottage cheese, cream cheese. In the back they would do it. And the fish, too, they used to smoke.

"Lottman's was built on the corner of Baldwin and Kensington. Oh, they had fantastic breads. They baked them with wood in their ovens and it tasted quite different—I still have the taste. Nothing compares to it because it had a different flavour. Even the bagels, you could smell them a mile away. When they baked the bagels it was all done by hand; it was like a ballet, they rolled it and they twisted it and used to put them on long poles to stick them into the oven, not in pans."

And Lunansky says the Kensington kids helped. "Well, we had to stand, and there were a lot of duties to take care of, maybe deliver an order or your parents would go and eat something so somebody had to watch, that's including all of us. It was a family affair, and we understood that we had to work." The adult work days started before dawn and ran until 9 P.M. or midnight, as long as there were customers. The Market closed early on Friday and opened Saturday night.

Frances Sanci Borg recalls, "On Saturdays everything was pretty much closed, and all the Gentile little kids, we would go, because the Jewish families couldn't open the lights on Saturdays or put on the gas, so they'd have these little girls go in and put the lights on and they'd give them a piece of honey cake or a few pennies.

"The Market was opened up again after sundown, and you'd be busy from seven. You'd be busy until midnight. And all the Jewish people would come here after the theatre with their gowns. It would be like a parade, and the streets were full of people, and they'd go shopping."

But it wasn't only food. Al Liebowitz, recalling the '50s, says, "Across the street next to Lottman's was Little Eaton's. He must have had a thousand and one different things. He would have nuts and bolts and kitchen gadgets displayed out front."

A neighbour says the store, which everyone knew as Little Eaton's, was run by two hard-working people whose primary transportation was a bicycle. "Every day he brought back something. The whole house, a two-storey house, was packed with stuff, in the bedrooms, under the bed, in the kitchen, in the stove. They had stuff stored down the laneway. He used to bring back big barrels on the bicycle. There wasn't anything he didn't have. The trouble was, when you went to get something, he couldn't find it."

Liebowitz adds, "Next to him, Ruminak, I think, he sold barrels and he would have empty barrels of all different sizes and shapes out on the sidewalk.

"There was the smell of meat, dairy, cheese. There was a fellow on Nassau and Augusta—Joe the orange man—and he would be out there shouting. You knew everyone on the street, there was no problem. I put my son outside in the carriage, and when he cried, people would walk in and say 'The baby's crying.'"

On Sundays in those days it was like the rest of Toronto—shut up tight. People remember buying an occasional milk or bread on a Sunday from a neighbour, peeking around the door as if they were in an illicit saloon.

On ordinary days, says Lunansky, "It was open late, and it wasn't quiet in one sense. It was more like a social club."

Mary Sokalsky Perlmutar remembers seeing her future parents-in-law sitting on the step taking the air at midnight outside their bakery.

Morris Perlmutar says his family kept a horse in a stable off Kensington. "We delivered to the houses. The horse knew where to stop for the calls."

There were several stables in the lanes around the neighbourhood. Mary Perlmutar's widowed mother, Rachel Sokalsky, was in the hay business for a while, her brothers driving the horse and wagon to deliver the bales. But horses definitely added their bit to the smells, the crowding and the clean-up problems.

People had coal and wood stoves and furnaces. Says Lunansky, "We had to put the ashes into bushels and boxes and bring them out to the front. And there was a day for the ashes to be picked up, and at one time it was horse and wagon. We knew the garbage person, he was a Scotch man with a moustache. He was a fantastic personality himself, with the horse and wagon. We used to have peddlers, the junk peddlers would come through the place with their horses and wagon to pick up all kinds of metals, and there were junk yards where you sold these things."

There were peddlers selling things, too, some of whom kept up noisy running arguments with the merchants, who didn't want the competition. Kids would sell strings of bagels. People brought in trucks on shopping days, parked them around Bellevue Square and sold produce off the back.

One of the Market's most venerable businesses began that way. Frances Borg, whose father started Sanci's, the banana store, says her family was partner in a fruit store at 47 Yonge Street. "Now in those days, we're going back to 1928, refrigerated rooms were almost unheard of. In the summertime if there were leftover bananas, he would just have to throw them out. So someone says, 'Well, why don't you go to the Kensington Market?' So he put some bananas on the truck and he came down to the Market and people were buying them off the truck—he was selling them very cheap.

"So he was doing this for a few weeks and then a policeman came by and he says, 'Well, you know you need a peddler's licence or you can't sell off the truck. So that's how we came to rent a place. When he had the leftover, my mother would sell them from the store."

Sanci bought a building on Kensington, put in refrigerators, and became the only non-Jewish merchant in Kensington. "All we sold was bananas because we didn't interfere with our neighbours, and they respected us for that and we got along fine with them. The first thing my dad did when he came in here he opened up a barrel of wine and he bought some beer and he called all the neighbours for a drink."

There were also *shochtim,* or ritual slaughterers, in the area. Lunansky explains, "They killed, and we used to have people that used to pluck the chickens. Elderly women used to come and pluck by hand. They would pluck the chicken for the customer, maybe get two cents, three cents.

Southeast corner of Baldwin Street and Kensington Avenue in 1919. Around the corner is an ice-cream store.

— CITY OF TORONTO ARCHIVES, RG 8-58-834

About 1922, customers for chickens at Morris Zamonsky's at 18 Kensington Avenue. There were several kosher slaughterers in the market and women who plucked the birds if you didn't do it yourself. — NATIONAL ARCHIVES OF CANADA, PA-084812

In those days it was precious, as a dollar went a long way. Then you would come back and pick up your chicken wrapped in newspaper, then you would have to clean it out yourself."

Garbage and smells were a perpetual problem. A man who left says his family looked at life in the Market pragmatically. "We knew living conditions were not the best. Most of us were fighting to get out of the area so at least you didn't have to go to bed at night smelling the garbage."

As Frances Borg says, "Chicken feathers were flying on the street, of course, and the smell of fish, but better to smell that than to starve."

Gradually the Jewish merchants changed the face of the Market. Not for the last time, much of what they did bent bylaws in this one-time residential area. From the 1920s on, there were more and more storefronts on the Victorian houses, more and more apartments upstairs, packed to the eavestroughs. In these small spaces lived parents, several children, grandparents and sometimes, as the children married, the new son- or daughter-in-law plus a roomer or two.

The three Perlmutar boys shared a room in the front of their building, listening all night to the *klink, klink* of the bakery equipment below. "The bakery was an addition to the house," says Morris Perlmutar, "and the brick oven was built then, 18 by 29 feet long. We had to use a 14-foot

pole with a shovel to get the bread out." His mother also used the stove in the bakery to prepare family meals.

Work there went on from about four o'clock in the morning until six or seven o'clock at night. And sometimes the ovens kept working after the people had stopped. "We would adhere to Jewish laws of not working on Sabbath. We'd finish our baking, then the women would bring their pots of roasts and bring it into the bakery." They would cook in the cooling ovens to be ready for the Sabbath.

Toronto's Health Department has been a frequent visitor to the market. This photograph was taken for it in 1934 at Groskopf Poultry behind 184 1/2 Baldwin Street.

— CITY OF TORONTO ARCHIVES, RG 8-1-1298

Ryerson Public School was opened in 1877. By 1914 the school was teaching manual training and domestic skills, new courses then, and offered a commercial course to teach office skills. The principal, William Groves, was quoted as saying the children came from poor and working-class families and needed training that would help them to earn a living as soon as possible, as few of them would go on to high school. — TORONTO DISTRICT SCHOOL BOARD MUSEUM AND ARCHIVES

Greenspan's meat store, in the Market from the 1920s, provided refrigerator space to customers who wouldn't have it at home.

During the Depression there were other kinds of commerce. Times were tough, and Canada's liquor laws restrictive. Bootleggers did business along Nassau Street, as they did in other parts of town. Neighbours recall a woman who ran a bootlegging establishment while her husband laboured in the needle trades. If the police called on her, her husband "sat for her," taking the rap so that she could stay in business. The kids in the area occasionally made a quarter carrying a bet to the bookies on College Street.

There were rumbles in the Market in the 1930s that reflected, sadly, the anti-Semitism of the times, when the Christie Pits riot took place and imitation fascists were patrolling the boardwalk in the Beach. Gangs would occasionally invade the Market looking for a fight. One man says the young men in the Market hid bottles they could grab as weapons if they needed them. A witness recalls with satisfaction that one fish merchant used a mackerel to smack an invader in the face.

It is also true that people in those very poor times looked after each other. Merchants carried customers. A family whose breadwinner was a railway porter, away weeks at a time, would get credit

The Ryerson
volleyball team
in 1928.

— ONTARIO JEWISH
ARCHIVES, 3182

Ryerson Volley Ball Team

Junior Champions Volley Ball League 1928

Max Applebaum,	Archie Atkin,	Sam Reindorf,	Jack Pollock,	Hymie Friedman,	Jack Weinstein,	Walter Karbownick,
Harold Reitaple,	Mr. Tobias, Coach,	Mr. Davidson, Principal,		Mr. Sager, Coach,	Sam Fruitman,	
Abie Cohen,	Louis Fruitman, Captain,		Jack Abrams,		William Mike,	

Photo by A. Art Gray & Co.

from store owners, then conscientiously pay it back when dad got home, using up most of that month's cheque.

Sam Lunansky says of his mother, "This house was always open to anybody. The kitchen went out to the street, on Nassau Street, and she would prepare food in the morning. She would go out very early and get the buns and the breads and put a pile in the middle of the table—coffee, cheeses, fish—and whoever came in ate. It was open always, she was very friendly."

Things changed after the Second World War, when the Jews began to move out. For a while the merchants stayed. Kosher-killed chickens were picked up in taxis to be taken north to Bathurst and Eglinton then Bathurst and Wilson in time for Sabbath.

But that was changing too as Toronto became home to more people from more places, and the big supermarkets began to carry a larger variety of foods. You didn't have to go to the market for your specialities. Merchants moved to where

their customers were. The few old merchants who remained became wholesalers to restaurants or went into new lines to attract the new customers.

Frances Borg says, "My dad died in 1948, then I pretty well managed the place. So we were in the wholesale business and times changed and small businesses were getting obsolete. By that time, things had changed, a lot of our neighbours had moved out and other neighbours moved in. But then I had an opportunity. A fellow from Air Canada came here and said maybe we would be interested in importing food from Jamaica. So he brought some mangoes down as samples and I put them in the store, and by that time there was an influx of Jamaicans, so they would come in and say, 'Oooh, mangoes, we would love to buy these.' So I was one of the first to import tropical fruits. Then we stopped wholesaling bananas because the big places were taking over, and we started in the tropical fruits. And that was in 1962."

Sonia Lunansky started Augusta Fruit about 1930, selling from a box on the sidewalk in front of her first home. When she died, the neighborhood named a park in her honour on Nassau Street. — COURTESY SAM LUNANSKY

Chapter 4 Helpers

Those who try to call Kensington a slum get a bristling argument, even from people who worked very hard to get out or to get their sons and daughters out. It is a community—a place to live and work, where neighbours help each other, and where they tell you with pride about the people who became super successful and moved on.

Still, if it has been a neighbourhood of opportunity and dreams, it has also been a neighbourhood of immigrants and of vulnerable people who, in the early years, worked long hours for little pay and no benefits.

One way or another, religion, social work and politics have been an active substream in Kensington, with three distinct sources. The first was the strong, traditional Jewish do-it-yourself style. Another rose out of the turn-of-the-century social gospel and the settlement house movement. The third one came during the '20s and '30s, with the buzz of the political left that surrounded Kensington.

The Jewish religious life began with a blossoming of small synagogues—congregations of people who came from the same areas in the old countries. They were used to a particular form of ritual, familiar dialects and customs. *Landsmenschaft,* that kind of coming together is called, and it operated in many ways in Kensington.

St. Christopher House in its final days, about 1973, at Wales and Leonard Avenues. The boarded-up houses on the west side of Leonard were soon to be demolished for construction of the Toronto Western Hospital power plant, stack and incinerator.

— *KENSINGTON ROOTS*

The Globe and Mail, Aug. 6, 1937

Toronto's Busiest Market On Kensington Avenue Has Asiatic Atmosphere

Interesting Assortment Is Offered for Sale to Tempo of Hucksters' Shouts and Babies' Squalls

A. LORNE MACINTYRE

Toronto's most congested market, the liveliest place of selling and buying of foods and merchandise is squeezed into the right angle turn of two streets—just where Kensington Avenue runs into Baldwin.

Here most any day except the Jewish Sabbath of Saturday and the Christian Sunday is market day. This, beyond doubt, is Toronto's liveliest. There's nothing like it any place else in the city, and it's more Asiatic, so it seems, than Canadian.

Panties and Herring.

With one hand you can reach into a barrel and pull out "fat pickling herring 6c." And, if you so desire, you can reach with the other hand at the same time to a pile of multicolored goods labelled "panties, per pair, 10c."

Trucks rumble down the street, halt, unload merchandise while the traffic jam grows and swells out behind them. Car horns blast and motorists yell. Dogs fight and kids scream. And above it all is the voice of a vender carolling, "Fresh fruit, fresh fruit. None but the best. I eat 'em myself."

Drygoods and Fish.

An ice cart swings into Baldwin Street and kids swarm about it, grabbing for handfuls. The iceman chases the kids, and pedestrians find themselves knee-deep in shrieking, jostling youngsters.

Noisy and Lively.

Thursday, when the heat of the afternoon sun lay in the narrow confines of Baldwin Street, hanging there between the shops, turning all the place into one long oven, the market was at its noisiest and liveliest.

Ancient women with shawled heads pondered and haggled over purchases. To any ordinary person all the fruits looked alike. But the buyers spend half an hour pawing over "cukes, 3 for 5" before finally extracting a nickel from a purse.

A fish stall sign says "carp 5c" and you can lift the carp alive out of a long tin box. A dozen of them are there in five gallons of water, waggling their fins. Maybe the last one in the box will have room to turn, but it can't while the others are there. Carp sell well. Whitefish is 16 cents a pound.

Street of Traders.

This is a street of merchants and traders. The names tell you that. Binstock, Winebron, Mintz, Herman.

Borsofsky has a house there. But what was once a four-foot lawn is now a fruit stall. If you don't want the fruit, Borsofsky has a sign on the house. It says, "plumbing and heating."

Merchants and traders down through the ages. Groskopf, Goodbaum, Seiden, Schwartz, Krabovsky, Leabowitz.

But the reporter wanted too much. He looked everywhere on the street. And he couldn't find a MacTavish.

from the Toronto Daily Star, 1970

"Kensington Market isn't romantic if it's your home"

Eda Shapiro lived in Kensington Market and hated it. To the outside, she says, it looks charming. But to the insider. . . .

I detest Kensington Market. Why? Because 10 of my formative years were spent in its squalour.

I have lived in Toronto most of my life, and with great pride I have seen it develop into an exciting metropolis. But I refuse to romanticise anything as ugly as Kensington Market. I take issue with these people who find the area so exotic and colourful.

I first saw Toronto as a 9-year old immigrant child, newly arrived from Roumania. My late parents decided to uproot our small family of four in order to seek a haven in Canada—a haven away from the growing anti-Semitism in Roumania.

I found Toronto impressive compared to the small Roumanian town we had left. The cold February Canadian weather was not unlike that of Roumania and presented no problem. My major problem was being unable to communicate. Though I spoke three languages fluently—Hebrew, Roumanian and Yiddish—I did not know one word of English.

My 7-year-old brother and I were enrolled in William Houston Public School (Nassau and Spadina), which is now a trade school. I had five years of schooling in an excellent parochial school in Roumania. But since my brother and I spoke no English, we were both placed in junior first (just one grade above kindergarten). This was embarrassing to me. But I realized that the lady principal had no other alternative.

When we first came to Canada, my educated and merchant father operated a grocery store on the south-west corner of Augusta and Nassau, which now is part of the "picturesque" Kensington Market. We barely eked out a "living," during the depression era. But it was the only solution for us. My mother was confined most of her 52 years to bed, because of serious heart disease. By toiling in that miserable store for ungodly hours (the days before early closing) we could at least have enough to eat, and also keep a close eye on my ailing mother.

Many a Saturday night I refused a date, to give my father some help.

The store across the street did a better business. They advertised their business in a barker fashion: shouting out their bargain prices.

For years I have deliberately avoided Kensington Market. Recently, out of curiosity, I returned to the area. This is what I found: The area is more congested than in the '30s when I lived there. The merchandise is displayed up to the sidewalk. Picturesque? The same is true of all the stores and stalls. I heard the same price hagling and barking.

At one store I saw a ten-year-old girl, Portugese, with a ready smile. I engaged her in a conversation. She was living poorly, and helping her parents. Suddenly the years rolled back, and I was that little girl. I had great compassion for her.

My feelings about Kensington Market have not changed.

Early St. Christopher House staff took pictures of the streets and yards around them, and of their young clients.

Top left: Denison Avenue.
Top right: Augusta Street.
Below left: Taken from St. Christopher House kitchen window.
Below right: Katerina Boere, winter 1915.

Some of the synagogues had started in the Ward. At first most were small establishments called *shtibles*. They were places of worship and study, schools for the boys, and social centres. The congregations had cemetery committees, and for a time were a resource for their congregations. There were members who would visit the sick, and funds to provide free loans to people in need. Jewish mutual benefit societies existed, often begun by secular Jews. Their membership was also based on common backgrounds, and members contributed what they could, which meant they were able to ask for help without embarassment if they were sick or out of work.

No matter who you were, to be sick and out of work in the first half of the 1900s was to have no income, no insurance, no hospitalization and, if the illness was serious, a good chance of dying.

One of the societies' benefits was the service of a doctor. The Jewish sick benefit societies hired young Jewish doctors who understood their patients, and who were being given a start in their practices. There were restrictive quotas on Jews in all of Toronto's professional schools and professional ranks for years.

Both the synagogues and the benefit societies were part of the social life. Members got together for picnics and annual dinners, for a much-needed chance to enjoy, to complain, and to share memories in comfortable company, away from the chronic strangeness and prejudice and the difficult attempts to gain a foothold. And the societies weren't confined to Kensington, some of them would grow and become part of evolving Jewish organizations.

At the same time, around 1900, all across North America and in England there were stirrings of social conscience. Churches, women's groups, and new social agencies were involved in efforts that would pave the way for public health-and-welfare programs. Their agendas covered poverty, the welfare of immigrants, public health, and child labour. Children's aid societies were starting, as well as health agencies and the settlement house movement.

St. Christopher House, which would be a force in Kensington for seventy years, was opened in 1912 in a large house at 67 Wales Avenue, then Bellevue Place, across the park from where the Denisons had lived and in neighbourly proximity to the shtible that would become the Kiever Synagogue.

The founders had looked for a downtown neighbourhood where they could establish a settlement house, found the vacant twelve-room Ryerson house built by Casimir Gzowski on Wales Avenue, counted one hundred children playing on adjacent streets, and set up business.

This man, Fichel Cooper, was a Pied Piper for the boys at Kiever Synagogue during the 1930s, taking them on outings, and encouraging them to maintain their Jewish faith and practices. — ONTARIO JEWISH ARCHIVES, 17

Settlement house workers lived in the house, as part of the neighbourhood. Sara Libby Carson, a founder of the movement and of St. Chris, defined their work as "just being friends to our neighbours." St. Christopher's old records have stories that illustrate what they did. For instance, there were two messages on the quiet Thanksgiving weekend when the 1918 flu epidemic came to Kensington. In response to one, St. Chris supplied food and a loan to keep a stricken family going until the father was well enough to work again. In the other case, they helped make funeral arrangements for a First World War veteran who died of flu "almost before his family realized he was ill. Its being a holiday made many difficulties."

A report in 1919 summarized the situation for many families, noting, "The average wage of $18 to $25 a week does not let people starve at all, but . . . so large a percentage of it goes on rent and fuel that you find continually badly nourished children and if their pride prohibits going to free clinics, it causes delay in sending for a doctor when a child looks ill and it necessitates getting the cheapest one possible. It necessitates mothers going out to work and leaving a ten year old child to look after the younger ones all day. . . ."

There were cases of tuberculosis, spread in crowded, dirty workplaces and homes that were jammed with people in every room. Then, the report described a client in the making on Leonard Street Rear: "Dear old soul in spite of drunken family life. A tragedy can be expected there at any time when they take to throwing lamps at each other."

But it was not all tragedy. Part of the goal of the social agencies in that period was to teach the women and children Canadian ways, to give them some skills and offer some social life. In that same year St. Chris had a morning playschool, an after-school girls' club, sewing, boys' athletics, a chorus, a social service club, nurse's consulting hours and English classes. Every girl in the sewing class made something she could wear. Preventive health care was also on the agenda—there were well-baby clinics, and women brought baby bottles every evening to be filled with pasteurized milk from the Hospital for Sick Children. There was summer day camp and a camp at Lake Scugog.

St. Christopher was supported by the Presbyterian Church, and by Sir James Wood, a wealthy Toronto businessman. Kensington was only part of the area it served; it drew people from blocks to the south and west. In 1920 it was estimated that 871 families and 1,500 individuals were involved with the agency. By 1930, 40 percent of its users were Jewish.

Top: In 1901, the Kiever Synagogue began as a part of a congregation in the Ward. In 1910, some of the members left to form their own congregation. In 1917 they bought the first of two houses standing on the site of Belle Vue, then bought a second in 1922. Four years later they hired a Jewish architect, Benjamin Swartz, to design the synagogue.

In 1981, it was restored with the help of the Ontario Jewish Archives Foundation and a provincial grant. In 1979, it was designated under the Ontario Heritage Act, the first Jewish historical building in Toronto to be designated.

— PHOTOS BY (LEFT) VINCENZO PIETROPAOLO, 2000, AND (RIGHT) WAYNE STARK, 1980

Below: Anshei Minsk congregation was one of the first founded in Kensington. Members worshipped first in a house on St. Andrews across from the present site. The synagogue was built in 1930, replacing two small houses.

— PHOTOS BY (LEFT) VINCENZO PIETROPAOLO, 2000, AND (RIGHT) RAY MCFADDEN

The Anglicans moved their mission to the Jews, the Nathanael Institute, from the Ward to Bellevue in 1916. This settlement house mission provided genuinely useful services with its message. It was home to Guides and Scouts, Red Cross meetings, English classes, mothers' meetings and after-school programs. A reading room was open long hours. In 1922, forty-three Jewish children attended the summer camp. The Institute used the gym at St. Stephen's Church, and in 1929 its boys basketball team won an Ontario midget championship.

A Jewish woman who attended in the 1930s recalls, "I know my mother didn't worry about it. The girls were taught how to sew, to cook. It kept you very interested. There were Hungarians, Ukrainians, Italians, Blacks—it was a very cohesive group." She says that as a small girl she tried to tell one of the staff she might be converted to Christianity, and the kindly response was that it wasn't likely and anyway, her mother wouldn't like it very much.

However there was no question of the Institute's goal. Said the church magazine, "The children are very keen to learn and we trust the seed sown in these young lives will bring forth fruit."

The agencies by no means touched everyone in Kensington. There were other outlets, for young people especially. Jewish boys went to the Young Men's Hebrew Association, the YMHA, on Brunswick near College, in the building that also housed the Toronto Hebrew Free School, now the Associated Hebrew School. There was a Jewish boys' club on Simcoe Street and a Jewish Cub troop at Orde School. William Houston School on Nassau was part of the playground movement that offered both recreation and training at schools, and in the '30s the city was full of sports leagues and competitions.

St. Christopher's would loosen its church affiliations as government-sponsored health-and-welfare programs started up, and city-wide fund-raising organizations were established to help support social agencies. In the 1940s the Nathanael Institute did some post-war ecumenical aid work for Jews in Europe, and in the 1960s it moved out of the area.

No neighbourhood exists without the outside world, and during the years before the Second World War there was another kind of faith that was part of the life of Kensington, the faith in politics as the cure for the ills of the world.

Spadina had emerged as the garment district during the '20s, and throughout that decade and the 1930s the street was in a chronic state of uproar, as unions organized and re-organized in a struggle to improve the harsh life of the people

who worked in deplorable conditions in the needle trades. From 1912 (when there was a failed strike by Jewish workers at Eaton's), there were Jewish leaders in the forefront.

Even if Kensington was primarily a living area and a market, labour and political battles went on all around it. Many of its people worked on Spadina and in the factories run by Eaton's, once the employer of three-quarters of the people who worked in the needle trades, and when there was a strike, it affected everyone.

As the Depression ripened and fascism rose, the unrest grew. March after march framed the area, across College Street and down Spadina, or up Spadina to Queen's Park. In 1933 about 15,000 people rallied to protest anti-Semitism in Germany. Political and union headquarters were on Spadina and Cecil Street. The Alhambra Hall, where endless meetings were held, was at 450 Spadina. And there was political theatre at the Strand at Spadina and Dundas.

The Labor Lyceum was opened in 1925, at the corner of St. Andrew and Spadina. Harry Simon, an organizer with the American Federation of Labor, said in a 1986 interview that the Labor Lyceum was a home for unions and the socialist movement, built on members' non-negotiable shares. The biggest was the Amalgamated Clothing Workers, but there were members there from leather goods, upholstering, and even a peddlers association that lasted into the 1940s.

"There were Jewish writers and poets," said Simon. "There wasn't a week when there wasn't some literary concert."

The Workmen's Circle originally encompassed all of the left-wing groups, but a split came in the 1920s when the communists were expelled. The communists then formed the Labour League, which became the United Jewish People's Order (UJPO). The League was a sick benefit society and cultural organization, as well as a political group. In a booklet published in 1936 to mark its tenth anniversary, it claimed a membership of "850 Jewish workers and progressive people."

A good many of the socialists and communists of the day were idealists, who believed that these political systems would do away with poverty and with the vicious anti-Semitism of the time. They were concerned with working conditions, unemployment, and old age pensions.

They created ferment far beyond their actual numbers, and were met with ruthless repressive measures that were protested by a few, but condoned by the broad community. A *Globe and Mail* editorial said that not all communists were Jews, but all Jews were communists, which added to the fear and hatred felt by many Canadians about the small group of communists in their midst.

The UJPO had a women's group, the Jewish Working Women's League, which in the 1920s led a successful strike against Jewish butchers, forcing meat prices down. Then they joined other women to take on milk prices, and won again. Like the social agencies, the leftists had youth groups that met all year, and summer camps started by the women's groups—the communist Naivelt (New World) near Brampton and the Workmen's Circle Yungvelt (Young World) near Pickering.

Al Soren, whose mother was part of the Jewish Working Women's League, was raised in the system. "In winter they had a Jewish school at Markham and Ulster. When I was a child I was a member of the Young Pioneers, the children's section of the Young Communist League."

מלחמה" מאכט —
אנפערינ-מערדער

מיר װילן האם
עמערע טאטעס מיט אונ
אונט אין דער מלחמה

When he was eleven he was chosen to go to
an international youth conference in Moscow with
a small group of American children. "That was my
life," he says. "That was how I was brought up."

Faith in the party lasted through the Second
World War, when Russia suddenly joined the
Allies against the fascist countries. Then in 1956 at
the Twentieth Congress of the Communist Party
of the Soviet Union, Nikita Krushchev made public Joseph Stalin's history of persecution and killing
of thousands of people, including Jews.

Soren says it was devastating. Joe Salsberg was
Ward 4's popular, long-time alderman and MPP.
His allegiance to communism had already begun

to waver, and he left the party after 1956, as did many others. Says Soren, "A lot of people were disillusioned with the disclosures, maybe ashamed that they were part of this. They felt betrayed. You spend a lifetime fighting for what you believe was a righteous cause, and you find it never was."

People in Kensington had spent the war years like any other Canadians, coping with rationing, with customers trying to wheedle an extra bit of meat or butter. Their children joined the armed forces, and they found full-time jobs after years of Depression-born unemployment.

Jewish families lost contact with relatives in Europe, and knew things were bad, but would not find out how bad until afterward.

Immediately after the war there were Kensington families who shared their homes with survivors who had managed to get to Canada in spite of immigration quotas. The garment unions brought others over, housing them temporarily and giving them work. They were given an exemption to the quotas because the industry needed people. Only a few years later, a wave of postwar immigration would begin that would change the face of Toronto—its makeup, its attitudes, even its eating habits—to make it as polyglot as Kensington. But Kensington would still be a reception area.

In 1956 a new group of Hungarians found their way there after revolution in their country.

A centre of Canadian-based help was the St. Elizabeth of Hungary Church, just around the corner at Spadina and Dundas. Peter Firkola, whose grandfather had come from Poland in about 1905, says, "There were three groups of Hungarians then: the old Hungarians who came in the '20s and '30s, the DPs (displaced persons) who came after the Second War, and others, like my dad who came to the Market in 1956 after the revolution."

So did Tom Mihalik's father, who opened a secondhand clothing store on Kensington Avenue. "My father was a peddler in Hungary, and he liked this area. We were at 54 Kensington Avenue, and on the same street we had the Litvaks, the Goodmans, the Daiters, the Lottmans and the Perlmutars. I grew up with some very hard-working people." He echoes the Kensington refrain. "There was a wonderful sense of community. The feeling was fabulous. You were a city within a city. You didn't have to leave Kensington Market. You had all your friends here and you worked here.

"And there was always something happening. After work you'd stick around for a couple more hours just talking to your neighbours. On Sundays you would get together with them and you would go on trips. We went to Sunnyside or we went up north or we went to a cottage.

The left wing helped foster Canadian Jewish culture. There had long been Yiddish theatre at the Standard Theatre and Alhambra Hall, not all of it imported. Then, during the 1930s, there was a theatre of action, making a statement about the times. In about 1925, the United Jewish People's Order started a folk choir, the Freiheit Gezangs Farein—in English, the Freedom Choral Society—most of whose members were factory workers.

Known during the 1940s as the Toronto Jewish Folk Choir, it performed at Massey Hall with soloists such as Paul Robeson. There was also a New Dance Theatre and a mandolin orchestra. In the 1950s and 1960s, a folk group called the Travellers was formed out of Camp Naivelt youth singers. The folk group were a well-known part of the leftist scene. — ARCHIVES OF ONTARIO, F 1405-23-119, MSR 9176, 36 PAUL ROBESON

"I didn't have a feeling that it was ghettoised, no, never that feeling. There was no reason. People made those stores, independent store owners made a fair amount of money for the hard work. You sent your children to school, they got a good education, and you made their future."

And the feeling of the familiar and the possible continued. A woman who had spent the war years in hiding in Budapest says, "It was comfortable and felt safe, everybody looked like me. We met friends and we went to the stores together."

She could find colours and designs in clothes and dishes that were familiar. There was a store that ground poppy seed the way she liked it, and sold the right kind of peppers. She shopped in Kensington too, to support the stores.

The Grossbergers came in 1958, with both the revolution and the concentration camps in their backgrounds. They knew no one. Says Morris Grossberger, "We spoke Hungarian, German and Jewish. When we first got here we wrote down every street not to get lost. But here is an international area, here in Kensington you can survive." They bought a store at Nassau and Bellevue, and were soon to find themselves surrounded by Portuguese. They developed a mixture of pidgin and sign language with their customers, found out what they wanted and brought it home from the wholesalers.

Toby and Nathan Gries on a sunny day in 1939 in Bellevue Park. Some local children recall a woman who lived on Bellevue who shooed the kids away if she thought they might trample the flowers in the formally planted park.

— COURTESY MARVIN GRIES

Left: Jack and Sammy Gelman in the 1940s. The Baldwin Seniors and Juniors were home-grown clubs formed at the YMHA on Brunswick to play a little baseball, and get kids off the streets. — COURTESY JACK GELMAN

Right: The Rakoffs, sons Al (left) and Sid (right), on Baldwin Street during the 1940s. — COURTESY SID PALMER

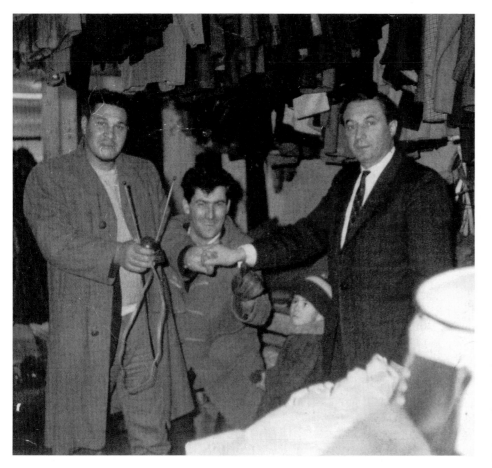

The Mihalik family arrived in Kensington from Hungary in 1958. William Mihalik ran William's Bargain, a secondhand store at 54 Kensington. Son Tom, now owner of Tom's Place on Baldwin, is drinking pop from Minnie's, the store next door.

— COURTESY TOM MIHALIK

By this time prosperity had taken many of the established Jewish families out of Kensington. One report says that between 1951 and 1961 the Jewish population dropped from 2,685 to 780. In the classic pattern of immigrants, they had begun to move north and west to newer, greener spaces. Their children, grown up and educated, built very different lives.

Drawings by artist Peter Matyas, a Kensington resident during the 1980s.

During the 1940s, artist Joe Rosenthal caught the essence of Kensington in charcoal-and-ink sketches.

Affordable housing, like these homes off Spadina on Glen Baillie Place, has attracted newcomers to Kensington since its beginnings. — PHOTO BY RAY MCFADDEN, 1980

CHAPTER 5 THE PORTUGUESE

There are places in Portugal and Brazil where Kensington is known as Augusta, pronounced mellifluously but something like *ow-goo-shtah,* because that street was the heart of the village the Portuguese created in Kensington.

Their arrival began as a trickle during the late 1950s, after a tussle between the two countries' immigration policies. By the '60s and '70s, Kensington was a major Canadian Portuguese centre. They became the new Kensington colony with a different style, but the same feeling of community.

Toronto's press was full of stories about what a change they had made. They painted the old house fronts in bright, warm colours, and decorated front yards with religious icons. Kensington bloomed with the grapevines and vegetables and flowers they grew in their backyards. "If there was a bit of soil," says Nick Da Silva, "we grew collards, tomatoes, salsa, grapes."

They also lived the life of immigrants, working hard, learning English and the new ways, and making their own home in the new world.

Isabel Gomes says, "People say to me, 'You are from Madeira Island? What are you doing here? Such a beautiful place.' I say, did the beauty feed anybody?"

Victor Pavao's mother began by cleaning chickens. "Mother worked in the basement of the poultry shop," he says. "You'd get ten cents a chicken, and it stunk. You put the chicken in the steaming water, pull out the feathers and singe it. She wore an apron and her own rubber boots." Then, like so many other Portuguese women, says Victor, she would clean office buildings in the evening. "My

The Tivoli Billiards Hall on Augusta and the Brazil Restaurant on Nassau were gathering places and informal hiring halls for Portuguese men during the 1960s. Photo taken in 1969.　　— PHOTO BY VINCENZO PIETROPAOLO

parents worked day and night. Dad washed dishes at the Ex, picked tobacco and worms. Scott Mission was where I got my clothes and my first skates. Three brothers all slept in one bed. We lived in the flat and downstairs was the live chicken shop. Part of the rent deal was keeping the chicken shop clean. We'd get our eggs out of the cages in the back."

Victor says the owner would leave pennies that the children could take to buy buns and candy.

He remembers, too, a wide-eyed small boy's personal culture shock at the sight of a ritual slaughterer, Zalman Weinberg, nicknamed Rasputin. "We had, I think it was nine slaughterhouses for the poultry in the area, and all the kosher slaughterers would come out, and it used to scare the hell out of me 'cause there was this one guy, he was huge, he was a big man and he'd come always with this bloody apron on and he had this scruffy beard, and I was terrified every time I'd see him."

By the 1960s Victor's parents had opened a store of their own, Casa Acoreana, which the sons still run. Victor worked there from the time he was ten. "At that time it was a really busy neighbourhood. The area was very different. There were trees in the neighbourhood. It looked different, it had a different feel to it. Everyday was like a Saturday. It had a hustle and a bustle to it."

The old houses filled up with new families doubling up and men alone crowded into shared rooms, saving money to bring their families over.

The Da Silvas shared a six-bedroom house on Augusta for a while, their third rented home in the area. There were sixteen people living in it, including four children, all relatives. There were two kitchens and two bathrooms, and the women all had their own kettles and cooked for their own families.

Isabel Gomes says she and her husband lived first in a rooming house on Huron, where the landlady restricted their use of hot water and charged extra for the use of the gas stove. They saved $1,000, borrowed another thousand and bought a house further down Augusta. "I was taking home $20 a week, my husband was bringing home $30. I spoke little English, I put my money in my hand so they can help themselves. At work, some of them called me stupid because I couldn't speak English. I said, 'Can you speak Portuguese?' After two years I have my sister-in-law and my neighbours and we had a party. We laughed, we danced and sang, we went into the park and danced. I always have nice neighbours."

The newcomers also helped each other. "One day we saw three guys sitting on the park bench," says Gomes. "They were Portuguese, didn't know where they were going, didn't speak much English. First thing, I make a big meal for them."

Then she put extra beds in a top-floor room where people could stay until they found a place to live.

Gradually the community took shape, and as the older Jewish families moved out, the Portuguese took over much of the Market, and the language of choice switched from Yiddish to Portuguese.

Says Gomes, "At the time the Portuguese people came, there was no Portuguese priest, no lawyers, but it was like a family. It was the Portuguese area. There was a Portuguese priest at St. Michael's, then they moved him to St. Mary's at Bathurst and Adelaide." She says she had been here for four years before the first priest arrived. "He was happy to see us."

The Gomes family turned the ground floor of their Augusta home into a store, and there were also the Melos and Salivera Markets, the Lisbon

Left and facing page: The Portuguese Book Store imported more than books and newspapers; it drew men to the corner of Nassau and Bellevue to listen to shortwave broadcasts of soccer games straight from home. Mario Tomaz put speakers outside to make sure no one missed a play.

— COURTESY TOMAZ FAMILY

Kensington was a major Portuguese centre for living, shopping and social and business life throughout the 1960s and 1970s.

— PHOTO BY *KENSINGTON ROOTS*

Bakery, and Vinga—warehouse and importer of Portuguese olive oils and tuna and frozen sardines and cod from Newfoundland. And there was Sousa's, which became the Brazil restaurant at Nassau and Augusta Streets, and the Portuguese bookstore, both magnets for newcomers.

Desi Gouveia's parents took over Sousa's, and, as the Brazil, it continued to be known in Portugal and Brazil as the place to go when in Toronto. The Gouveias also ran a rooming house next door that had a laundry in the basement. The restaurant and the Tivoli pool hall were informal hiring halls for people looking for work.

Desi, one of eight children, says for his first ten years he was brought up by the older ones. "Mom got up at eight and went to bed about one. The restaurant was open 365 days a year. We couldn't go anywhere. It was a friendly atmosphere. The clientele were all Portuguese speaking. It was a little world of its own."

The Portuguese Book Store drew Portuguese from all over the city and the suburbs. The Tomaz children, who moved the store to Dundas and Ossington when the centre of Portuguese life moved, say, "Some of the people in Kensington never really learned English. Everything they needed was there, and they worked in factories with other Portuguese." The business began in a small way. "At first Dad brought in a few Portuguese

— PHOTO BY VINCENZO PIETROPAOLO, 1969

The Gomes supermarket on Augusta, 1981. The family followed Kensington tradition, getting their start by opening the store in the front of the house. — PHOTO BY VINCENZO PIETROPAOLO

Top: Manuel, Augustino and Isabel Gomes in 1977.

— COURTESY ISABEL GOMES

Below: Starting from scratch, making wine in the basement, are Jōao and Tiago Alves, Carlos Gomes and Carolos Alves.

— COURTESY ISABEL GOMES

newspapers and sold them at the house, then at the Lisbon Bakery at Oxford and Augusta."

When the store was opened, Mrs. Tomaz ran it, and her youngest child, Jose, says he was raised there. "People came to the store for information for jobs and a place to live."

In 1974 there was a revolution in Portugal to overthrow the fascist government and, says Mary Betty Tomaz, "Suddenly there were newspapers about all the parties, left-wing parties to right-wing parties, and I remember there was this big political thing in the bookstore. People would fight, some would want to buy a communist newspaper and ask to put it in a bag so nobody would see. Any opposition to the fascist government was considered communist." Some of his customers wanted Tomaz to stop importing some of the papers, but, as his kids say, "He wasn't a communist or a fascist and he wouldn't exclude any newspaper. Papa was North American style. He didn't exclude any newspapers. 'This is Canada. It's a free country.'"

He also started something that's one of Kensington's legends. He delivered another touch of home that brought dozens of Portuguese men out into the streets every Sunday to hear shortwave broadcasts of the soccer games. He'd hang a loudspeaker outside the door, and the men would gather to cheer on their teams. "Every Sunday, that

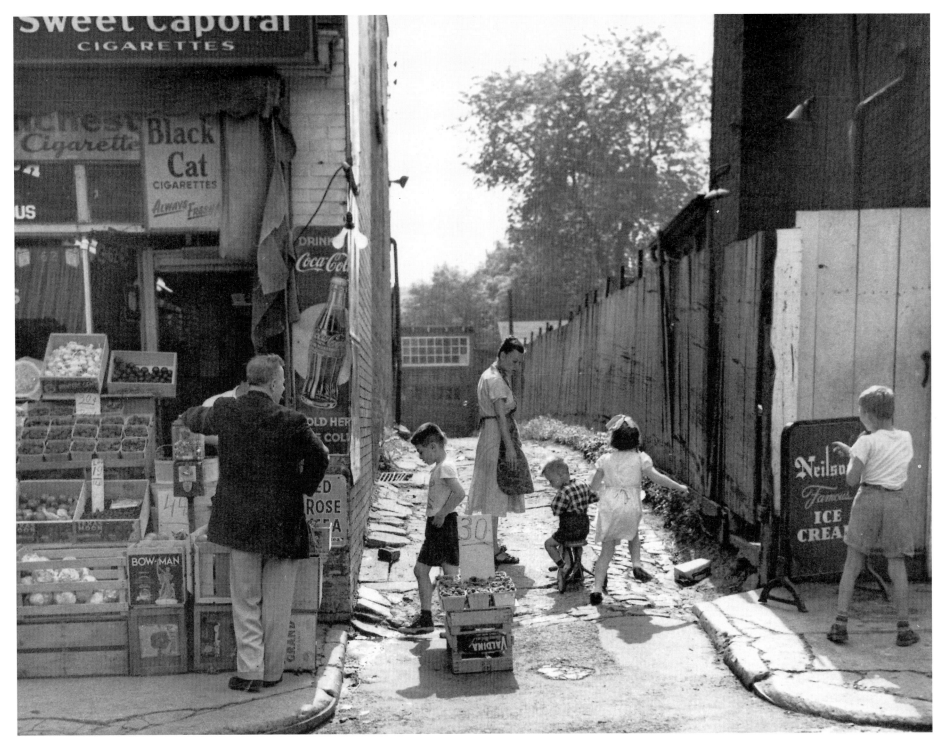

Facing page: Looks like a call home for lunch in 1955 for children playing in the laneway beside Leopold's fruits and vegetable store.

— MICHEL LAMBETH, NATIONAL ARCHIVES OF CANADA, PA-178393

would happen, every Sunday," says his daughter. "He'd put it so loud outside people who were not Portuguese would call because of the noise. The police were always good, they were very polite about it because they understood."

Once or twice big-name soccer players from Brazil or Portugal would drop by the store, to the delight of their Canadian fans.

Tomaz and Gomes were both founding members of the Portuguese Canadian Club, which was housed for a while in a small building at Leonard and Wales. It was a men's club, but it was also a school. Tomaz imported textbooks from Portugal, and at the Portuguese Canadian Club and in homes around the area there was after-school Portuguese school to teach the children something of their parents' language and country.

There were also the city-wide Portuguese Business Men's Association and the umbrella Portuguese Canadian Congress that would provide funds for advanced education, and most of their members were in Kensington.

For the most part the social life centred on the family; on gatherings in one another's homes, on the verandah, or in the backyard during warm weather. There were card games, gossip and song. Nick Da Silva remembers the men doing what he calls duelling with lyrics—improvisational singing. It was intense, he says, as each man waited his turn and thought about what he would sing.

Jenny Tomaz recalls, "There'd always be a fado. Fado means faith—it's a way of singing about life and loss, about love. It's beautiful. It's usually sad because the Portuguese have always emigrated, they were sailors."

During these years Kensington was minutely examined by all kinds of government bodies, and one of the facts that emerged was that there was a high population of children. In 1975, 35 percent of the people in the area were under nineteen, and 27 percent were under fourteen; there was a very active children's life. They worked—Kensington kids have always worked—in the family stores and restaurants, in other people's stores and restaurants. But work was not all there was to it.

"It was a wonderful time," says Victor Pavao. "I really enjoyed it here in the Market. We'd go to the wading pool and my Mom would buy doughnuts and bring them to us. We played from morning to evening. We'd climb fences and go in people's yards. You were in the neighbourhood. People knew us, and no one would give us a second thought.

"When we started playing ball hockey we organized street teams and Baldwin Street would play Markham Street, and we'd play Euclid and Palmerston. Each street would have its group of boys.

"Stan the cop, he would come into the shops and talk to everybody. He would never take stuff

This and facing page: Kids have always worked in Kensington Market—if not in a store, there was always some other way. One veteran of the Depression set up an orange crate on Baldwin to sell shoelaces. Another, who worked for his family in those days, remembers buying one ice skate from the junk dealer next door and buying the second one a month later when he could afford it.

— PHOTOS BY VINCENZO PIETROPAOLO

Two Da Silva boys on Bellevue. Across the street is the since-demolished manse of St. Stephen's Church.

— COURTESY NICK DA SILVA

rink. We'd flood it. It was really pretty good in terms of racial harmony. The big thing was, were you a good hockey player? If you were a good hockey player it didn't matter what else you were.

"We used to play in the Market every day, play hide and seek, running through the area. We used to hide in a couple of shops, hide under the fruit stands. As long as we didn't break anything or disturb the customers, nobody minded. It was a great place to play." He remembers the chickens as their own little zoo, the Kensington zoo. "We weren't conscious of the cruelty," he says.

Betsy Tomaz agrees. "The Market was so colourful. I just loved the chickens, and I remember the pigeons. I'd buy a pigeon and bring it home and it would peck holes in the bag. Dad raised them for fun. But there were a lot of cats and raccoons and rats, and raccoons just slaughtered all the pigeons."

Jose Tomaz says, "I remember walking out and there would always be someone to play with. When we'd get tired of playing we'd go to Mr. Grossberger's variety store and eat ice cream and sit on milk cartons outside the store. We made up a ball hockey league. In front of my Dad's store was one team's home ice and Kensington school was another and the parking lot down the street was another. We were the Oxford boys and the Bellevue boys. Dad made prizes and he would post

for nothing. The cops would ask us if we had any money. 'How you gonna call home if you have an emergency? If you've got no money, go home.' There was an unwritten curfew for young kids."

Says Peter Firkola, "There's a parking lot on Bellevue next to the synagogue, and in the evening when it was closed we would just bring our nets. It was a nice flat surface. Across the street was a patch of land from Bellevue to Leonard—it was the soccer field, the football field, and the hockey

up the standings at the store so all the kids would go check out the standings and the top goal tenders. We lost to a team called the Jets."

Desi Gouveia remembers, "I was brought up here from day one. As a teen I knew everyone, every nook and cranny. I didn't feel threatened. I even knew the drug dealers. I felt safe. I knew nothing negative would happen."

But Tomaz sounds the neighbourhood theme. "One of the facts I like about Kensington is that I can identify with an actual neighbourhood with actual boundaries. I like the fact that my neighbourhood had a name."

Arnold Winn recalls child mischief from a few years earlier. He says there was a barn just west of Denison, on Dundas, and an ice house just below Wales that backed onto it. The kids would "gee-up" the horses, hitch a ride behind in the winter, and hang around to get small chunks of ice off the back. He says in warmer weather, merchants would cover fruit and vegetables with a canvas and hire someone to watch it at night, but that didn't stop the youngsters from raiding the stands for an apple. He was also part of the organized young life of the schools and social agencies, and remembers it with pleasure. There was a church basketball league in Toronto, and in the 1950s, a Black drum corps.

"We were the Toronto Negro Trumpeters, TNT; our logo was exploding dynamite," he recalls. " We practised in a band hall in a laneway behind St. Stephen's. Went to Washington, DC, to represent the Elks, opened the Oshawa shopping centre, we were in the Santa Claus parade. At the high point we had about one hundred kids."

Winn was number seven in a large Black family that lived on Wales Avenue. His mother grew up on Bellevue, and he followed in her footsteps at Ryerson School. When he went on to Harbord Collegiate, it was about 95 percent Jewish, and closed on the Jewish holidays. "We'd just go and sign in and go home—had the best of both worlds. I went to St. Chris from nursery school. We couldn't have survived without it: it kept us off the street. It had a games room, woodworking, Friday-night teen dances. It was a place where musicians came to jam, and we would go and listen.

"The U of T would send its social work students, coming down to work with the poor, underprivileged kids. We'd laugh."

He says the only problems he had were with newly arrived immigrants. "We had several Black families at Ryerson, and at St. Chris we were all colours, all backgrounds. If there were problems, it was with the new people. The kids within the neighbourhood were so used to each other."

Bob Ellis made his way to St. Christopher's from a few blocks west. He became a volunteer,

The young people in the TNT (Toronto Negro Trumpeters) lead a parade. At the height of their success, they had about a hundred members. — COURTESY ARNOLD WINN

and then a staff member. In the 1970s, recalls Ellis, both St. Stephen's and St. Christopher were running sports programs for the young people, some of them from Alexandra Park, south of Dundas. "To give them a focus to their lives, and a leadership program. We used every facility you can imagine—Lord Lansdowne School, Ryerson, Kensington School, George Brown College, a church at Bathurst and College. We were masters at finding places where we could take the kids. The high-profile program was lacrosse. It drew kids from Kensington, Bellwoods and Alexandra Park."

Ellis's predecessor, Bob Opperman, is a Native Canadian who started the team, even making some of the equipment and repairing the sticks. Volunteers also raised funds so the team could travel. They made it to Northern Ontario and to Victoria for a major tournament.

"The parents were working hard; they didn't have vehicles," says Ellis. "Our kids used to be considered orphans by the other teams. They thought they were orphans because they came in a big van with me and other volunteers."

Ellis also says there was an occasional hassle with league officials over fighting. "We were so diverse in our makeup and that was a problem. We'd run into a little racism. I said, 'We come from a mixed community and our kids aren't used to being insulted because they're Italian or Portuguese or Jewish or Black.' You just don't do those things, because that leads to pandemonium. But for the most part, the young people remember those times fondly."

There were about 4,000 Blacks in Toronto during the 1940s, most of them living from Spadina west, roughly along Dundas and College to Ossington. Black families had the United Negro Improvement Association at College and Augusta. The UNIA had its roots in radical politics. It was the centre for activists working to improve the lives of Blacks, notably railroad workers and domestics. But like so many other Kensington area institutions, it also served as credit union, meeting place, concert hall and information and housing centre.

The Kensington connection was no accident. In an era when even well-known Blacks were refused rooms in hotels in Toronto, they could find rooms in Kensington. Some Black organizations allied themselves with Jewish groups to strengthen unions and social causes.

"That was another neat thing about the area," says Ellis. "It was quite complex, and lots of pockets of activity. It's a must for getting in touch with an old part of Toronto. You get a real sense of the diversity of the community."

Led by St. Stephen's Community House, Kensington helped save the Doctors Hospital in 1976. Humberto Medeiros speaks at a rally at the Kensington School. — COURTESY ST. STEPHEN'S COMMUNITY HOUSE

Beleaguered, embattled and fighting mad, Kensington residents had an astonishing ten years or more of political warfare in the 1960s and 1970s, from which they emerged victorious, with their neighbourhood intact, in spite of governments, developers and encroaching institutions.

They all had agendas that seemed reasonable to them, but which did not reckon with the opinions of about 5,000 real people who were living in a vibrant neighbourhood that was being threatened by outsiders. The people of Kensington are passionately protective of their village, some because they need it, some because they love it.

How fiercely was a lesson learned the hard way by any number of politicians and planners during those turbulent years. Citizen groups formed and re-formed, sometimes in tandem with Kensington's business people, sometimes against them, but always determined to preserve their homes and neighbourhood against a formidable array of foes.

The forces that would have diminished or demolished Kensington included the Spadina Expressway; the Urban Renewal Program, as proposed by a coalition of federal, provincial and municipal governments; the expansion of the Toronto Western Hospital; the expansion of the University of Toronto for a married students' residence; the expansion of the Provincial Institute of Trades, which became George Brown Community College in 1968; the Toronto Board of Education, which wanted to build a new school; and the merchants in the Market itself, yearning to grow to meet a new, fashionable interest in the area.

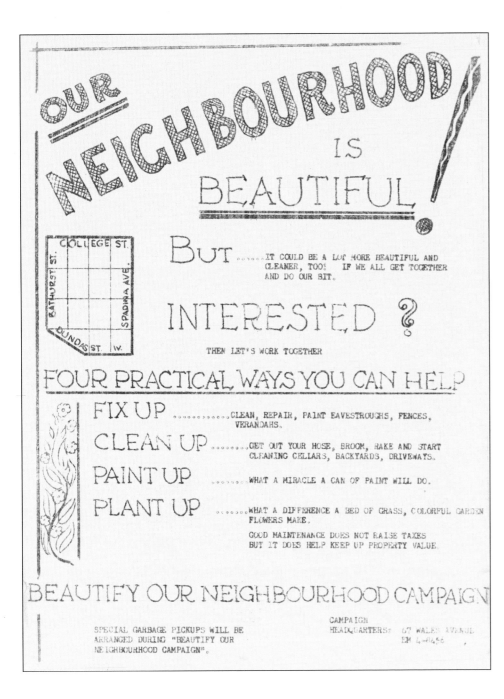

Beautify our Neighbourhood Campaign

Press Release

A Committee of interested neighbourhood residents, businessmen, Churches and institutions working together with common concern for the improvement, beautifying and betterment of our neighbourhood by encouraging individuals in our area to "Plant Up, Paint Up, Clean Up and Fix Up."

Left above: A headquarters was set up at 110 Oxford Street as an information and meeting place during negotiations for Kensington Community School.
— TORONTO DISTRICT SCHOOL BOARD MUSEUM AND ARCHIVES

Below: Former Mayor Phil Givens, Sammy Luftspring and Alan Grossman at a 1980 St. Stephen's party marking the publication of *Kensington Roots*.
Luftspring was a Canadian boxing champion whose autobiography included the story of his boyhood in the Kensington area. — *KENSINGTON ROOTS*

Right: Alice and Dan Heap with young friend Riel Lawrence. Dan Heap was first alderman then MP for the area including Kensington. Alice was second chair of the board of St. Stephen's Community House . — COURTESY ALICE HEAP, PHOTO BY MARTY CROWDER

All except the merchants had expropriation powers and each brought the area to the brink by threatening to exercise them. The key was the Urban Renewal Program, in which all three governments were involved. Under it, the area was a target for total redevelopment, like the area south of Dundas, which is now Alexandra Park.

The force that fought back was truly grass roots. It was the people of Kensington, of every background, led by doughty warriors including David Pinkus and the late Alan Schwam, and supported by the social agencies, notably St. Christopher House as well as St. Stephen's Community House and the Portuguese Social Service Centre.

And they didn't do it all in a vacuum. Those were activist years, when the voice of the citizen was heard in Toronto. The "Stop the Spadina" movement was headline news, fighting the threat of a huge expressway cutting south through the city to the Gardiner, chewing up neighbourhoods with the ramps it would have taken to feed it. If Kensington had survived the coming of the expressway, it would have survived in its looming shadow.

Rev. Dan Heap, who moved into Kensington in 1968, would become alderman and then MP for the NDP in the area. He says Pinkus and Schwam helped to form the city-wide Confeder-

ation of Residents' and Ratepayers' Associations (CORRA), of which Schwam would become vice-president. Both Schwam and Pinkus were long-term residents of Kensington. As a young man, Schwam was among the left-wing radicals; he worked as a journalist, trained as a town planner, and taught at York University.

Pinkus, a professional engineer who had served on staff at the University of Toronto, was deeply committed to his community, serving on boards at St. Christopher House, Western Hospital and Kiever Synagogue.

Citizens set up the Kensington Area Rate Payers' Association (KARA) to hold block meetings and to create their own plan for redevelopment, and the city established the Kensington Urban Renewal Committee (KURC) to help determine renewal policy. It was a city council committee, headed by Controller Margaret Campbell, and included the area's two aldermen, as well as Kensington business people and residents.

Campbell, who was a firm ally, was quoted as saying, "Our wealth as a city is in communities like Kensington. The whole of the Spadina area, too. People are worried about the whole thrust of the Spadina Expressway. People are asking, 'What is the plan for the south of Bloor?' Well, in Kensington, if the Western Hospital expands

During the 1970s, while Kensington was striving to stay alive, Spadina was beginning to see changes, as many of the old Jewish stores and restaurants became home to new Asian establishments.

— E. R. WHITE, CITY OF TORONTO ARCHIVES, SC 118-869

eastward, the expressway goes right through and the school expands south . . . then there won't be much left."

Says Pinkus, "Eventually the feedback came from the people, saying, 'We don't want it. Please go away,' to the chagrin of the planners who had all sorts of plans."

A story in the *Toronto Star* in July 1969, said, "City planners had been thinking about making it [Kensington] the object of an urban renewal plan since about 1957, but didn't actually do so until 10 years later. Urban renewal in Toronto and elsewhere had sometimes been like a red rag to a bulldozer—an invitation to wholesale clearance. That was exactly what the people of Kensington didn't want.

"The greatest worry of the people in Kensington was that property would be expropriated. Western Hospital, the University of Toronto, and George Brown College had expropriatory powers and could well make their wants felt in the course of urban renewal.

"And just to the south of Kensington, in Alexandra Park, urban renewal had meant a big public housing project—a project that was thought to be one of the best looking in the city,

Signs of change at 33 Kensington Avenue.

— PHOTO BY RAY MCFADDEN

Special delivery at the corner of Nassau and Augusta, 1970s.

— TORONTO DISTRICT SCHOOL BOARD MUSEUM AND ARCHIVES

Perlmutar's Bakery on Baldwin Street in 1972. Like most Kensington stores, it was an add-on to the house, and the family lived upstairs. — ONTARIO JEWISH ARCHIVES

The last board of trustees of Toronto Western Hospital before its amalgamation, first as part of Toronto Hospital, now the University Health Network. David Pinkus is seated fourth from right in front row, Delphim Viana is second from right in back row.

— COURTESY DAVID PINKUS

but one that all the same they didn't want reproduced in their neighbourhood."

Alan Schwam spelled it all out in a retrospective column in the *Kensington Market Drum* written in 1989. "In the spring of 1967, the people of the Kensington area were informed by a letter from the Mayor's office, City of Toronto, that a 'study of your neighbourhood' would be carried out, lasting one year, which would 'lead to a program to improve the condition of houses, stores, streets, sidewalks, parks, parking and the features of the area.

"The May 2, 1967, study signalled Kensington's entry, along with about 20 other communities in Toronto into a class of 'substandard' neighbourhoods designated as 'urban renewal' or 'urban renewal study areas'."

A 1963 City of Toronto Planning Board report on priorities for Urban Renewal Study Areas included six areas on its hit list. It estimated the population of Kensington in 1961 at 5,494, and the average income a low $3,318. It also said that 22 percent of residential structures were in poor condition, and that traffic conditions were poor.

Wrote Schwam, "In the whole city south of Bloor Street, from the Don to the Humber Rivers, people were in a state of shock and confusion. Few dared to put a penny into the upkeep of their homes or businesses because along with urban renewal came the dread legal weapon of expropriation whereby anybody's property could be taken away from them as long as it was for 'public purposes' . . .

"To combat this situation in our community, KARA was formed in September 1967 at a meeting attended by over 300 people in the old St. Christopher Settlement House.

"Only a month later the first significant victory was achieved when the area's MPP Allan Grossman made this historic commitment at a

public meeting during the 1967 Provincial election campaign. . . ."

Grossman was the Conservative MPP for Ward 4 and a cabinet minister. On October 12, 1967, he said, "You are going to have a great deal to say about how your own district is going to be developed. The Ontario government is going to refuse to participate in any kind of urban redevelopment until it is satisfied the people not only know what is going on but they will be represented on the committee which makes the decisions."

A formal version was read into Hansard and became government policy, known as the Grossman Commitment.

Schwam wrote, "The 'Grossman Commitment' was no accident. Its terms had been worked out in several face-to-face meetings between the minister and members of the KARA board. . . . It took much hard lobbying and many meetings before that election promise was transformed into government policy." (That promise was to be cited in legal arguments by residents' associations across

Kensington principal-elect Lorne Brown (wearing glasses) and social worker Bob Marino (with beard) walked and talked around the neighbourhood, listening to opinions about the proposed community school.

— TORONTO DISTRICT SCHOOL BOARD MUSEUM AND ARCHIVES

Toronto.) "KARA and the Kensington Businessmen's Association took the initiative . . . Between April and July of 1968 a 14-point program for the residential portion of the community had been approved by the KARA executive, translated into Portuguese and prepared for circulation to every home in the area. A short time later a similar 14-point program for the Kensington Market area had been prepared and widely circulated."

It was adopted by a committee of council and council itself, and then there was a pause. Schwam concluded, "It took city hall staff thirteen years to incorporate the program into an official plan for the community."

Then there was Toronto Western Hospital, which Pinkus describes as growing like an amoeba. It had a long history in the area, dating back to 1899, when it bought property that included the MacDonell farmhouse. Pinkus says it was always welcome from a health point of view and as an employer, not in the medical practice area, but in low-end jobs. But it has not always been a comfortable neighbour.

It had grown several times, notably in 1957, when half a block of houses and stores was demolished for a hospital parking garage and medical office building privately owned by the doctors. "I'd been critical of the expansion plans, which

would have absorbed Bellevue Avenue," says Pinkus. Shrewdly, and in response to neighbourhood pressure, he was appointed to the hospital board, and in 1974, became chair of the building and development committee.

By then the Grossman Commitment was a factor. Dan Heap was quoted in the *Star* as saying, "When we came to buy here [on Wales Avenue] we were warned about expropriation. My own doctor at Western Hospital has told me the hospital will have to move this way.

"But then we heard about this provincial commitment. People bought because of that commitment. They fixed up their houses because of it."

As a community representative, he went to discuss the situation with hospital officials, and was told that he was raising questions that really should be settled by elected representatives.

The next time he went he was alderman for the area.

"The struggle to keep it from expanding north, east and south was quite a struggle," Pinkus says. "Kensington became a hotbed of community activity as an impediment to some of the plans of the planners of the city."

In 1968 the University of Toronto's part in the drama began, when it bought a 1.2-acre block of land with $525,000 granted to it by the province.

Says Pinkus, "We fought the university too. The block on Oxford Street and Bellevue, Lippincott and College was up for development, and the Student Administrative Council of the U of T had acquired it. SAC had a wonderful scheme planned. They were going to build a housing project and it would be Rochdale number two. Rochdale was a social experiment that went wrong. The Portuguese who lived in that area were very disturbed by the drug scene, and said, 'We don't need this next to us on our block.'"

At a meeting held in May 1968, a representative of SAC said they wanted to build a project for 700 people. Pinkus responded that that was a "phenomenal density" compared with the surrounding usage.

He explains that it was also regarded as an intrusion into the area, because it could have led to further expansion of the university's boundaries, which had not then extended that far west.

Opposition to KARA appeared in *The Varsity*, the University of Toronto's student newspaper, in a 1969 article accusing Schwam of being a power broker, working secretly with a developer with plans for the land. And it said the Portuguese were not represented in KARA until Controller Margaret Campbell ordered it.

Then everything changed suddenly, recalls Pinkus. "Almost overnight the Student Adminis-trative Council decided to get out of it, and they sold the land to the board of education, which was a broken commitment."

The Toronto school board paid $601,000 for the property to build a new school, and for a while things looked worse. At a meeting with the urban renewal committee the board said it actually would need twice as much land for the school; that would mean expropriating as many as thirty homes.

No one doubted a school was needed: there were thirty-four portables at the existing schools in the area—Ryerson, King Edward and Lord Lansdowne. Twenty-two of them were at Ryerson. What people did question was the need to demolish so much of the neighbourhood.

There was even a proposal for satellite schools to be scattered throughout the neighbourhood in existing buildings.

Says Heap, "The school board had a very simple plan. You tear down all the houses on the east side of Lippincott, the north side of Nassau and the west side of Bellevue. Then you have a proper-sized school yard. We had meetings and meetings."

What Kensington finally proposed was a community school—a new idea at the time. "We went to the school board and I was surprised at how much support we got," says Heap. "The board did an extraordinary thing: they hired and appointed a principal before the school was built." He was quoted at the time as saying he was so surprised that he was "light-headed."

Lorne Brown, the principal, and Bob Marino, a board social worker who spoke Italian and Portuguese, set up headquarters in a house at 110 Oxford Street, and the community was canvassed and canvassed again about what it would like. Brown says, "My first job was to establish some kind of credibility. The citizens of Kensington were very suspicious of the board and quite convinced that I was there to get them placated and calmed down."

They called it a charade, a mockery, and said Brown already had the school plans in his hip pocket, and formed the Kensington Citizens' Committee, chaired by Murray Starr.

The meetings and door-knockings went on for a year. Brown met his neighbours, listening to old stories, playing dominoes on the front porch, playing his guitar and singing old labour songs in the living room. One day he and Marino made sure everyone knew about a meeting by driving around the neighbourhood while Marino stuck his head out of the sun roof and announced it, shouting through a megaphone in three languages.

The architects' plans, which took the citizen recommendations seriously, were submitted to a meeting and approved. The neighbourhood fin-ished with a smaller school, with only two buildings on College Street torn down. Part of the playground was on the roof, and the building was in scale, looking like a small apartment house. In the front corner on College was a community space that would be much used, and which was for a time home to the Portuguese Free Interpreter Service.

The summer before it opened, the new teachers, hired specifically for that school, went around the neighbourhood to introduce themselves to the children they would teach. Brown recalls that it took on a Pied Piper look, as the children began to follow their teachers from home to home.

But there was also another ingredient in the stew, as tensions between the residents and the Market boiled up. There were new and different merchants, and a new influx of shoppers. The Market, which had for years been mostly on Baldwin and the north end of Kensington, was spreading, down Kensington and all along Augusta, encroaching more and more on the residential streets.

David Pinkus says, "As the community changed, one of the threats was Kensington Market, a tremendous resource, but there were problems associated with garbage, noise, smell and traffic. There was always this latent turmoil between them. There was a cleavage between the

In 1972, No. 8 Hose Station burned in a huge blaze that brought out a lot of Toronto firefighters and all of the Kensington neighbours. The bells plunged to the bottom of the tower during the fire. The tower itself stood, but was so weakened it had to be taken down for safety's sake. The station was rebuilt as a replica of the original.

— *KENSINGTON ROOTS*

Market and the residents, but a mutual obligation, even if we quarrelled about the boundary lines." The crux of the problem, he says, was stealthy growth. "The Market was not entirely kosher in terms of its expansion. There were a lot of scofflaws."

Heap says the Market had always grown informally, and the growth was gradually legitimized by spot re-zoning after the fact. "There were some remarkable weekend conversions from residential to commercial. I was quite impressed by how fast they could build. People would build and they'd be faulted for building illegally, then they'd get it legalized. After some more of that they'd say, 'Well, why not the whole block, why can't it all be commercial?'"

With city help, houses had already been torn down for a parking lot on Bellevue and a garage on Baldwin that runs through to St. Andrews. "It was partly a matter of keeping residential streets between Augusta and Bathurst from being totally dominated by parking for the Market," says Heap.

If the problem has never gone away, it has been slowed by constant alert opposition.

KARA was truly a Kensington group. Says Pinkus, "It was a wonderful group, a mélange of individuals. Guys like Ed Clarke, who was Black and one of the heads of the United Negro Improvement Association, was also vice president of KURC. We had Dan Martyniuk, an electrical contractor who lived on Bellevue and was a Tory party supporter; Delphim Viana, an electrical contractor; Americo DeSousa, a pastry chef; his wife Ophelia; Tony Vaz, a tool and die maker and community worker; John Moran, a construction foreman." Judy Ramsay, a community worker from St. Christopher House, was a major organizer and facilitator, and the late Ophelia DeSousa is credited with being an opinion shaper who encouraged Portuguese parents to be active participants in the endless discussions about the school and later in parent groups.

It was a group that was feared at city hall, says Pinkus, adding that similar things were happening in Trefann Court and Don Vale.

Alice Heap says, "There was a considerable remaining population from before World War II with very close bonds and a willingness to organize when it was needed." Dan Heap adds that Pinkus and Schwam "were quite firm about saying neighbours are neighbours—Jewish, Portuguese, Chinese, Anglo—they are neighbours."

Quotes in local papers provide a good idea of the feeling that was behind all the hard work.

Clarke said to a *Star* reporter in reference to urban renewal, "The officials are thinking again about buildings, not people. This is the last true cosmopolitan principality in this city, a place where many people from many lands have homes together."

DeSousa said, "There are people here who will get a new immigrant a job, will get him credit, will get him a place to live. If the government has any concern at all, for this reason alone it should keep Kensington alive."

In a story in *The Globe and Mail Magazine,* Delphim Viana was quoted as saying, "If we lose this community, we are lost. We depend on this community to succeed in life and work in Canada. And for our older people it is like home. My mother can shop at the market and she can go around the corner to our own church. She is happy, but if the community was destroyed, she would be destroyed too."

In June of 1971 the Davis government stopped the Spadina Expressway at Lawrence Avenue. In 1969 the federal government shut down the urban renewal program and its funding. George Brown didn't expand in Kensington, but expanded by way of satellites in other parts of the city. There were some trade-offs with the hospital, allowing it to grow upwards and downwards without expanding its acreage. Housing was built on some of the land it had taken over, including the old home of St. Christopher House. St. Chris moved out to a new space on Augusta in 1973, and then out of Kensington to continue its work south and west of the area. The hospital sold its venerable Wales Avenue location to the city, which replaced the worn-out buildings with public housing.

The Kensington school was shown off as a pattern for future citizen participation in schools. Across the city, reform candidates were elected to municipal office, as they had been for years in Kensington's ward.

Says David Pinkus, "It was a magic time. We didn't realize it during those day-and-night meetings. We changed the hospital—we changed the area. We influenced the construction plans for future schools, and re-focussed the city's vision of the preservation of its neighbourhoods. Without a doubt we saved the Market as well as the area."

Traffic has always been a bugbear in Kensington's old streets. All kinds of solutions have been suggested, but so far none has worked. — 1980, *KENSINGTON ROOTS*

There's a school of thought that holds that the Market area has never been the same since its squawking symbol, the chickens, were banished. That was in 1982, after City Council passed an animal control bylaw that forbids the keeping of live farm animals within city limits. The Kensington Businessmen's Association fought it. Its chief gadfly and sometime president, Gus Fisher, was quoted as saying, "One girl who was vegetarian passed through the market and saw in the crates too many chickens and she call the health inspector."

The merchants asked for an exemption. They claimed selling live birds was a long-standing Kensington tradition and a distinctive part of its cultural diversity and its tourist appeal.

"How is wringing a chicken's neck an expression of cultural diversity?" questioned Neighbourhoods Committee Chair Dorothy Thomas, and the chickens were history.

There were other signs of change in ever-changing Kensington all through the '70s and '80s, as it was discovered by the young and with-it. In Bellevue Park for a while there was long-haired radical chic during the days of the hippies and with the arrival of Vietnam war protesters.

In the Market, Stuart Scriver and Pat Roy were harbingers of the times when they opened Courage My Love, a funky new version of the old junk stores. They moved into Kensington in the late 1970s, at the beginning of the booming market for near-antiques and old clothes dubbed vintage and therefore fashionable. Both had been teaching at Kensington School, and they started their business on Cecil Street, combing the area for the saleable contents of old stores and houses.

Joe Oksenhendler in Louie's Coffee Shop in Kensington in the 1970s. His father took over the shop at 197½ Baldwin Street in 1962. Louie and Dora Oksenhendler arrived from Germany in 1961.

— PHOTO BY MORRIS MILLER

Scriver describes their start: "Because we didn't really have a lot of money, and we discovered that people had an awful lot of stuff being tossed out that was still good. We drove down to Queen Street and drove along looking for old stores going out of business."

The next year, in one of the many stories done over many years on new faces in Kensington, a newspaper article listed their new-wave neighbours: a store carrying beaded silk and cotton outfits; the Vinyl Museum, selling old records; Sun Ra Natural foods and XOX Artists' Postcards. Though they shared the same old Market, they were a far cry from kosher butchers or Portuguese fish stores.

Kensington had become hip, and a target for tourists. "Where in Toronto," the story asked, "can someone shop for groceries and then recuperate outdoors over a 'cosmic' sandwich, tofu burger or curried goat with a ginger colada while enjoying reggae or folk music—all in the space of two blocks?"

West Indian bakeries and food stores had appeared on demand, with patties and produce from Jamaica and Barbados. Yvonne Grant opened Caribbean Corner in 1980 while the chickens were still clucking. She says there was never a concentration of West Indians living in Kensington, but they enjoyed shopping there because, like so many others, they could find familiar things to buy, among them live chickens. "There were Muslims, Indians from Guyana and Trinidad who wanted the chickens Halal killed."

Carol Wong, who ran Screenplay, selling her own designer clothes, was quoted in the *Globe and Mail* as saying, "It's artistic and earthy here, not like the Eaton Centre." It attracted young artists of every kind.

Says actor Ray Landry, "It was definitely the place to start in the city. You paid $450 for a three-storey house. When you were cooking you shopped by the hour; if people dropped in, you went and got something else." And even those sojourners fell under its unlikely spell. "What I remember," says Landry, "is that once you got inside the market you were at home there, you were in a different place. I always felt safe there."

Above and top right: Harry and Faye Daiter ran a dairy store on Kensington Avenue from the mid-1930s. In the late 1950s, Faye presides over a counter where goods sold for prices very different from today's. The family lived in the apartment over the store.

— COURTESY RON DAITER

Below right: In the 1960s, what may well have been a final appearance by a horse in Kensington. — COURTESY RON DAITER

Across the street, Joanne and Keith Harburn were running a bed and breakfast, and, for a while, a restaurant. "It was affordable and comfortable," says Joanne. "There's an essential goodness here."

The safety and essential goodness slipped a little during the late 1980s, when the area became infested with drug dealers and developed a reputation that kept people away. The *Kensington Market Drum,* the community newspaper, complained that mainstream media coverage was adding to the problem: "Because of superficial and irresponsible media coverage, Kensington has in the last few months been used like a film set for stories on something that is a city-wide problem. The immediate result was that the number of prospective drug buyers in the area increased dramatically."

The story is that the residents helped to clear out both buyers and pushers by taking pictures and noting licence plates, and by asking for unpredictable and visible policing.

They got a lot of help from young punkers, who moved around from Kensington Avenue to Baldwin to Oxford and operated out of spots variously called Fort Goof, Goof's Tower, and Goofworld. Goof Steve Johnston says the punkers started their own anti-drug campaign. They sold pins that read politely, "Coke: The Real Thing for Real Fools." The punk group centred on a successful band, and they put together a drug awareness event in Bellevue Park, mixing reggae and punk music with talk about community action to win back the streets.

In spite of its new stores, the Market continued to be under attack from city authorities about its collective congestion and hygienic habits. And the mythical vegetarian girl wasn't by any means the first to invoke the health department. In the early '60s, politicians had toured its streets to investigate complaints from residents of unsanitary conditions. A *Star* report said Alderman Harold Menzies stepped on a dead rat and proclaimed indignantly, "We should bulldoze the whole place out of existence. It's picturesque, but it's grotesque."

There were a number of official reports that said querulously that the city gave the merchants more cooperation than it got in dealing with the chronic parking and health issues. A 1964 report pointed out that the city had done its bit by expropriating twenty-four residential properties to create two parking lots, spending two million dollars on a parking garage, and providing extra street cleaning. It described the Market as the "only intensive retail area not located on an arterial street," which has always been at the heart of the problems.

Ten years later, still at it, a Department of Public Health report deplored hygienic conditions,

Mrs. Citron, mother of Augusta Avenue's egg lady, Zippora Offman. — PHOTO COURTESY KIRK CHENEY

Kensington has always been valuable as a starting place. As each new wave of immigrants has arrived, the traditional ways of shopping have helped them to feel at home. — PHOTOS BY VINCENZO PIETROPAOLO

especially in connection with the six remaining kosher chicken slaughter houses. "Cooperation with this department," it said, "is less than ardent."

Totally unrepentant, Kensington merchants went on fighting city hall. And in 1988, Gus Fisher led the merchant troops in an old-fashioned shindy over canopies. Fisher is from Yugoslavia. He began by selling potatoes wholesale, opened a store in the Market in 1958 and came to own a great deal of property there. He was a leader in the Kensington Market Businessmen's Association from its beginning in 1962, and a thorn in the side of one city council after another. He has fought for parking, for sidewalk improvements, against urban renewal, for the expansion of the market, and for canopies.

Since the 1960s, merchants had been encroaching on public sidewalks, expanding their stores inexpensively by building canopies. The Public Works department opened this skirmish by saying the canopies were non-conforming. They didn't meet a bylaw that said anything attached to the front of a store has to be "temporary, unenclosed and easily removable."

Consumers Gas then entered the fray. It said there were gas mains under some of the canopies, and that could be dangerous in case of a gas leak. Well, said Fisher, then move the gas mains.

Kensington Avenue, east side, 1981.   — PHOTO BY VINCENZO PIETROPAOLO

Left: In the 1970s, West Indians came to Kensington for mangoes, patties, ginger beer and music.

— PHOTO BY VINCENZO PIETROPAOLO

Above: Tiger Armstrong, who ran Tiger's Coconut Grove, a cafe on Kensington, created a typical Kensington tempest in 1984 when he asked for a license to use his five-by-six-foot sidewalk space as an outdoor cafe. There was opposition from the neighbours and a noisy meeting of about seventy people, which culminated in the license being granted. Tiger's did not have a liquor license.

— COURTESY RAY LANDRY

Consumers Gas said it would, but it would cost over a million dollars.

Then, according to a story in the *Kensington Market Drum,* "Fisher now was in his element—the bureaucrats had accepted his argument in principle—yes, we can move the gas mains instead of demolishing the canopies. It's only a matter of cost and who gets to pay that cost."

This went on for three years. Said the *Drum,* "Only the mains on certain sections of Augusta would have to be moved; certain sections of the main were 50-60 years old and would have to be replaced anyway . . . with each little detail, the costs came down and down: from over a million to a quarter of a million, to under a hundred thousand, to forty-five thousand."

The finale was a triumph of chopped logic. Consumers' Gas moved the mains. City Council approved retention of the canopies and there was a suggestion that the whole operation be paid for with the money merchants paid the city for the encroachment on city property, that is, for the canopies.

In the 1970s, a passing cat keeping a hopeful eye on Max Stern in Max and Son Meat Market. You never know your luck.

— *TORONTO SUN*

And there were other issues in the area during the '80s and '90s—there are always other issues. Toronto Western Hospital wanted to expand again, and there was a dispute about its incinerator, smoking with contaminants from medical waste from several hospitals. It took several years before the incinerator was closed in 1997.

Another revitalization plan was shepherded through city council by an alderman, the late Dan Leckie. A year later George Brown College moved out, and that set off a whole new debate. The college property was eventually bought and converted to condominiums by a private developer. It is one of several changes involving housing in the area, and gives rise to concerns that this time the very heart of Kensington might change if it becomes gentrified.

Says Maria Santos, who was born in Kensington and who works at St. Stephen's Community House, "The type of building going up does have an impact on the fabric of a neighbourhood. Historically this has been a place of acceptance of people who were not accepted elsewhere. All types of communities have been accepted. People want to keep that culture."

Live chickens arrive in Kensington in 1977.

— TORONTO STAR SYNDICATE

The view from inside the Oxford Fruit store, at the corner of Nassau and Augusta, where grapes are hung in the Malaysian tradition.　— PHOTO BY VINCENZO PIETROPAOLO

In the meantime, Kensington's surround had changed beyond recognition, as a new wave of Asian immigrants enlivened the existing Chinese area on Dundas and built a new one along Spadina, turning the old Jewish stronghold into something very different.

Within Kensington, the new immigrants bought businesses and houses and definitely became part of the mix. But as always, it's different, says Tam Goossen. "The Chinese community in here is quite diverse. I'm from Hong Kong. A number of people on this street are from China and from Vietnam. One of the great contrasts between newcomers like ourselves and the Jewish residents is that there was a real sense of community for them, even though they came from different places. The fact that there was a religious life, economic life and social life all in one area contributed to that sense of community, whereas I'm afraid the newer communities don't have that."

Which is not to say they haven't taken an interest. Goossen and her husband, Ted, moved in in 1970, and she became involved with the Kensington Community School, which their children attended, and was then elected school trustee.

The early days of the Kensington school coincided with a drive for heritage language classes in Toronto schools, in which children could learn the languages of their parents' countries.

Says Goossen, "There were some really active people who pre-dated me. There was a very active Chinese Parents' Association, not a school-based one, but an area-based one. Well, they were fighting for Chinese language classes, and they tried to bring our Kensington parents to meetings and

Mildred Morris (third from left) and Capt. Don Paterson (standing, right) taught an early version of English as a Second Language at St. Stephen's Community House in the 1960s. — COURTESY CAPT. DON PATERSON

The Portuguese Nazaro Folk Dancers won first prize at a Freedom Festival in the 1960s.

— COURTESY CAPT. DON PATERSON, PHOTO BY CUSTODIA PHOTO STUDIOS

—*Custodia Photo Studio*

ST. STEPHENS—The Portuguese Nazare Folk Dancers, above, won first prize at the third annual Freedom Festival this spring and appeared at the CNE in the fall. They are one of many ethnic groups reached by St. Stephen-in-the-Fiel's, where the rector is the Rev. Canon Guy Marshall, as it tries to help new Canadians to feel at home in their new land. This colourful and talented group meets regularly at St. Stephen's Community House where, directed by Capt. Don Paterson, CA,

there is a full recreational program for adults and children of the neighbourhood regardless of background or creed. About 300 persons weekly, including children and teen-agers, and representing 16 national groups and 12 religious and denominational backgrounds, use its facilities. Two of these groups took part in the closing grandstand show at the CNE this year. From meetings at this Community House has come forceful representation designed to make much-needed improvement in the standard of housing in the area.

During the 1970s, St. Stephen's began sponsoring street festivals that seemed to involve everyone. Then Mayor Art Eggleton opens a festival on Bellevue Avenue outside the community house.

— COURTESY ST. STEPHEN'S
COMMUNITY HOUSE

talked to the school to make sure that the Chinese parents' concerns were taken into consideration.

"It was not a single community issue, it was a real coalition of the immigrant parents. The Chinese parents worked with the Greek parents and the Black parents and the Portuguese parents, and this whole coalition demanded that the board provide these programs, and they got support.

"It was golden days for real community involvement with the school board, and it was all

immigrant groups. Everybody remembers those golden days. There was a real sense of affinity between, say, the Black parents and the Chinese parents."

In Kensington, she believes, there is more than one reason for this affinity. "It's a bit of a class issue as well, because the people here are not as affluent as everybody else. There's a division. The line is drawn at College Street, and south of College the houses are smaller and it's working

St. Stephen's seniors, pictured here at the annual United Way Walk-A-Thon, are enthusiastic participants in activities in and out of the House. — COURTESY ST. STEPHEN'S COMMUNITY HOUSE

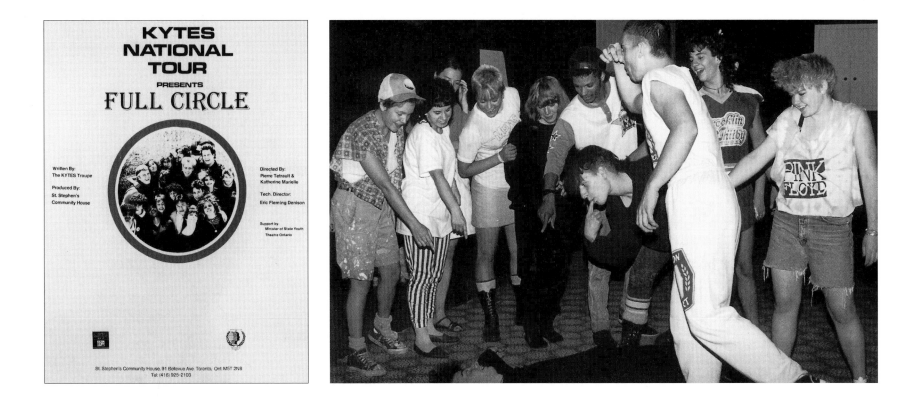

KYTES - Kensington Youth Theatre Ensemble of St. Stephen's, was founded in 1983 and sponsored by the House. It is an innovative program that uses threatre as a tool to help troubled youth reconnect to their community. Productions are written by the participants and address issues that are relevant to their lives."

— COURTESY ST. STEPHEN'S COMMUNITY HOUSE

class. People have a general acceptance of working-class values, although they're not going to be upset if you're going to move ahead and become somebody else. There are people who are middle class, and they just live quietly with their neighbours.

"There is a mixture. But it's not just ethnicity, there is that class awareness. There again I think it's a contribution of the Jewish community; they laid a rather interesting tradition. It was a real hotbed of activism here."

Yvonne Grant takes up the familiar theme of the affinity that comes with everyday Kensington

life. "It's a good mixture because you learn a lot of stuff from a lot of other cultures. Now we have more Asians, more people from Somalia and Sudan, even some from Iran and Saudi Arabia. People speak Chinese to me and I don't know what they're saying, I know a very few words. They come in and buy rice from us because I think they feel comfortable. If they come more than once, I tend to know what they want. Sometimes I ask them what it looks like and get them to draw it for me."

As both Kensington and Toronto's wider community were absorbing new people, St. Stephen's

Community House was evolving into a new-style centre to meet the social and economic changes the '80s and '90s would bring. During the '60s and early '70s, St. Stephen's was a magnet for young people, affectionately known as the House, and officially reporting to the Anglican diocese and St. Stephen's Church. In fact, it was one of Kensington's usual anomalies. It was run almost independently and on a shoestring by Captain Don Paterson of the Anglican Church Army and by his wife, Ethel.

It was the gathering place for organized groups such as the Scouts and Guides, a place for troubled young people to find help and a friendly drop-in for kids from Kensington and beyond. It was open long into the evening, and Paterson estimates there were sixteen nationalities represented among its children and teenagers.

Peter Firkola says it was almost like a family-run centre, not very organized, but a good place to go. Paterson trained promising youngsters to become volunteer leaders in their teens, and Firkola was among them. "Every Saturday morning we used to run a program for a lot of those kids seen by teachers as trouble makers, outcasts. We did sports, trips, camping—basically showing them respect and offering a positive influence."

Mildred Morrish, paid by the government, taught English there from 1964 to 1976, with assistance from Paterson. St. Stephen's provided child care for the mothers in the class. Then the '70s brought a sea of change. After ten years of virtual non-stop work, Paterson resigned in 1974, and the church considered closing St. Stephen's. Rev. Campbell Russell, then rector at the church, pleaded for time to re-create the agency, because he felt that it was needed.

There was the brief dream of a multi-purpose centre. In 1978 the Sisters of St. John, who operated the Church Home for the Aged two doors south of St. Stephen's, moved to another part of the city. They had been on Bellevue for seventy-two years. Says Russell, "We had a vision of tearing the whole block down and rebuilding the whole thing to include both the church home and community outreach. It was to be a terrific combination."

But the Anglican church said there wasn't enough money; it had to be either/or. "Well," says Russell, "there wasn't any question in the Church's mind or anybody else's mind, it was the community house."

The sale of the old home made news. It became the property of the Unification Church in Canada, nicknamed the Moonies after their wealthy Korean leader, Rev. Sun Myung Moon. A *Globe and Mail* story at the time said it was sold first by the Anglican church to the president of a

Everyone gets into the act at a 1990 Kensington community festival.

— *KENSINGTON MARKET DRUM*

construction company, then resold a few weeks later to a vice-president of the Unification Church in Canada. He was quoted as saying the building was bought in his name to avoid controversy. The Moonies, said the *Globe* story, "were accused of brain-washing and holding young people in church training centres against their will."

In any event, says Russell, there was consternation in the community and a sigh of relief when the Moonies left after about ten years. In 1992 the building was bought by the Homes First Society and renovated to be used as affordable housing.

Homes First worked with St. Stephen's, hiring unemployed workers from their programs for the project.

Overseeing the shift of St. Stephen's from a church operation to community centre was Brian Smith, who began his work on a budget of $17,000. Partly to make the money stretch, he and his wife and young family moved into the house, as the Patersons had done. When they moved out three years later they probably ended a chapter, making Smith the last settlement house worker in Toronto to live on the premises in the way the founders had years earlier.

For a while they shared quarters with Sister Brenda Duncombe, who became the community worker for St. Stephen's. The first thing they all did was paint and repair the house.

In the spirit of the times, the second thing they did was ask the neighbourhood what they would like the community house to do for them. The reply was provide a day care where the Portuguese could speak in their own language to the people looking after their children. The day care opened in 1974, and by the 1980s St. Stephen's was working with King Edward School to expand it and add languages.

In 1974 St. Stephen's Community House was incorporated. The church kept a connection, but handed over the building under the auspices of

St. Stephen's Property Corporation. This St. Stephen's became a United Way agency in 1975 and recruited both staff and volunteers from the area, adding programs to work effectively with the people around them.

Says Russell, who was chair of the first board of the re-constituted St. Stephen's, "We didn't want St. Stephen's to be a bureaucracy, we wanted it to be a community house." At first they had a board that represented three language groups—Portuguese, Chinese and English. That meant board meetings that went on until midnight while everything that was said was translated twice.

In the interests of efficiency, they organized grass-roots groups that would make plans, which were then okayed by an officially unilingual board.

In about 1976, Brenda Duncombe, with Portuguese- and Chinese-speaking colleagues, went out again to survey the neighbours. "We arranged walks around the neighbourhood. Just going into the house and speaking Portuguese . . . it just made all the difference."

This time the request was for English as a Second Language (ESL) for both Chinese and Portuguese. "The first class had just five students, but I could feel it growing," says Duncombe.

The St. Stephen's staff made a difference in ESL. For example, Duncombe says they discovered that immigrant men were given precedence in ESL

classes, and they worked "wholeheartedly" to have that changed. Then she and her colleagues began working with their students in a way that is still practised—they encouraged people to talk about their opinions, about the cultural differences they were coping with. They also invited local aldermen into classes and built into their English classes some practical awareness of Canadian politics and social life and how they work.

Duncombe also became an advocate for individuals, straightening out large problems and small, usually with bureaucracy of one sort or another. Earlier she had tried to help people take

Brenda Duncombe (centre) shares a party with students from her ESL classes. She helped pioneer a new approach, combining an introduction to Canadian social and political life with language instruction.

— COURTESY BRENDA DUNCOMBE

advantage of a funding program to renovate the old houses they lived in, but with limited success. "The government was demanding quite a lot from the people themselves, and they hadn't got the money."

She and a colleague, Sidney Pratt, encouraged Portuguese women to join the unions at their factories. The growing, changing list of things St. Stephen's did reflects what was going on around them, as more new people found Kensington.

The late 1970s and '80s were the years when refugees from southeast Asia were arriving, some of them the so-called boat people. Programs were developed for Chinese seniors, for Chinese, Vietnamese and Laotian families, and for young refugees from southeast Asia. In the late '80s there were refugees from Latin America, and a program in Spanish for them. The agency supported the Columbian and Chilean Associations and the Portuguese Democratic Association.

Also in the '80s, Ruth Morris, a Quaker and an activist, was program director. She took St. Stephen's into pioneering work in conflict resolution. Now volunteers trained by staff help people, often from different backgrounds, solve problems by helping them to understand each other. The approach has had international recognition and has been the model for similar programs in other cities. It has also become a fund-raising

enterprise for St. Stephen's, teaching the techniques to professionals and business people.

In 1976, St. Stephen's was a leading player in the struggle to keep the Doctors Hospital open when the provincial government threatened to close it. It was seen, says Smith, as the immigrant hospital, and although not in Kensington, it served many of its people, with its range of languages.

But the rescue was temporary. In the late '90s, the Doctors Hospital was folded into Toronto

A lament for the chickens in a Kensington Carnival Arts Society production at the Theatre Centre in 1990.

— *KENSINGTON MARKET DRUM*

Western, which had been folded into Toronto Hospital. The building was torn down, to be replaced by a long-term care facility, but St. Stephen's is still working with its new incarnation as the Kensington Health Centre.

For several years, from 1975, the agency published *The Kensington,* a newspaper in English, Chinese and Portuguese. It told people about resources, where to get help, and what was going on locally, and its editorials got down and dirty, supporting neighbourhood causes. For instance, in 1976 there was talk of building a senior citizens' residence that was considered inappropriate for the area. When its opponents, the Residents of Kensington Businessmen's Association, reached an agreement with the city to scale it down, the Kensington Business Association took issue, because they wanted stores on Oxford Street.

The Kensington's front page item began, "Well, Gus Fisher, you have really done it this time! After months of ROKA working on a senior citizens building that would fit into the character of Kensington the whole project may be lost because of a failure of the executive of the Businessmen's Association to accept the city's decision on zoning. . . . The city has just confirmed that Oxford is for houses." St. Stephen's and ROKA won this one.

That same year they joined forces for a fund-raising street festival that signalled the beginning of an array of Kensington festivals held ever since. They closed the street from College to Oxford, even commandeering the lawn at the Home for the Aged, whose residents loved it. There was something of everything—Portuguese food, a Chinese lion dance, a Chilean dance group, local school bands and choirs, an organ recital in the old church, tours of the fire hall, a guitar and

Ida Carnevali, founder of the Kensington Carnival and the Festival of Lights.

— COURTESY IDA CARNEVALI

banjo duet by MPP Larry Grossman and Kensington School principal Lorne Brown and a street dance at night.

St. Stephen's gave up its festival in the late '80s, and became a sponsor of a wider festival ten years later as Kensington partied on. The festivals are a new kind of citizen participation, filling the streets with parades and the park with bands and artwork and children's entertainment. By the '90s the summer festival featured twenty bands and twenty more acts, and was attracting 10,000 people. In 1992 there was a mammoth outing to raise funds for people burned out in a fire on Kensington Avenue.

In 1983 Ida Carnevali moved into Kensington. She is a clown, a director and writer, and founder and artistic director of Kensington Carnival. She says she loved Kensington for its European feeling and because, "In markets, it's always theatre, there is an interaction between people." Another chicken mourner, she says, "There were still live chickens and live rabbits and all of that. When that was outlawed . . . it was a big loss in the karma of Kensington."

She began her Kensington career with street theatre in the park. "The chickens became our mascots, so we made all these chicken masks and costumes and people would run around as chickens in the parade.

"I called it Kensington Carnival because a carnival is always very eclectic. You can have theatre, you can have music, you can have sideshows, you can have puppet shows—anything."

For two years the carnival included a *son et lumiere* history of Kensington that became a theatre production, but her company's most colourful contribution may be the Festival of Lights, which winds its way south through Kensington from St. Stephen's Church to celebrate the winter solstice.

A visitor who came unexpectedly on the event wrote: "I fell into a pan-religious celebration of the solstice. It was a strangely joyous and zany parade, mostly in costume, through one of the older districts of Toronto."

His account, reprinted in the *Drum* in 1989, went on. "Before friends and I gave up the parade because of the severe cold, we had dancingly witnessed a pagan ritual of the victory of good over evil, complete with a fire breather, witches, a snow queen and children bearing roses; a Christian scene which I could not see because of the crowds and a telling and singing of the Hanukkah story with flaming torches."

That year the celebration finished with a feast put on by the Toronto Tai Chi Association at Cecil Community Centre, with steel band music and a Mexican pinata filled with toys for the children. When there was food left over, it was taken to the

In 1998, Toronto Mayor Lastman, who grew up in Kensington, did a walkabout through the area and met Frances Borg of Sanci's, a boyhood neighbour and friend. — TORONTO STAR SYNDICATE

nearby Scott Mission to be used on the coldest night of the year.

Christina Chu Schwam believes that that spirit of inclusion is what has made Kensington matter. She believes it explains why people like her late husband, Alan, have loved it and fought to keep it alive against some fierce odds, and why it has been so important for immigrants. It's been Kensington's role, she says, to do the mixing.

"It is the story of the immigrant, from one group to another group to another group," she says. "Kensington is a marketplace. The essential shops are there, the bakeries are there, the meat stores are there, the fruit stores are there, the vegetable stores are there.

"The sense of everyday living is in there. People from all walks of life, from all cultures will go in there. It's a common daily routine for individuals.

"Now the difference between Kensington and Chinatown is in Chinatown you see Chinese faces. You walk into Kensington you really have a mix—you see a mixture of faces. You see the people who have been here for a long time, the people who are new. You see people who are white, people who are not white. That mix is there, and . . . the area has allowed that mix."

Left: Kensington has long been a subject for stories, photographers and filmmakers. From 1975 to 1982, the CBC ran a popular television series called "King of Kensington," starring Fiona Reid, King Al Waxman and Helene Winston.

— CBC DESIGN LIBRARY

Right: During the '90s, actor-writer-director Don McKellar's "Twitch City" was filmed and produced in Kensington.

— PHOTO BY CYLLA VON TIEDEMANN

Kensington Photo Essay by Vincenzo Pietropaolo

Over the years Vincenzo Pietropaolo has returned, time and time again, to Kensington with his camera. In 1981 he photographed every building in the market. The images in this photo essay offer a glimpse of the day-to-day life in the market and surrounding community.

Delivering pigs to a Portuguese butcher shop on Augusta Avenue, 1990.

Girls playing hopscotch on Augusta Avenue, 1981.

Joao Rocher in his backyard on Casimir Street, building a model Portuguese fishing boat, 1995.

Left: At the corner of Kensington and Baldwin, 1969.
Right: Selling blankets and sleeping bags on Kensington Avenue, 1981.

Left top: This migrant farmworker from the Caribbean would regularly accompany his employer to sell farm-fresh vegetables on St. Andrews Street on Saturdays, 1981.   Left below: Greek butcher shop on Baldwin Street, 1991.
Right: Maria Sandu and Lucero Lopez in the store on Baldwin Street, 2000.

Left: Kensington, seen against Toronto's downtown skyline, is obviously out of a different era. If you look up past the storefronts you can still see its Victorian origins.

Right: St. Elizabeth of Hungary Church, at the corner of Spadina Avenue and Dundas Street, just before demolition in 1985.

Rayne behind the counter at Courage My Love, a funky store on Kensington Avenue, 2000.

European Meats on a busy Saturday morning, Baldwin Street, 2000.

Two shops on Augusta Avenue, Segovia Meats and Harry David, 1995.

Mariano Maiato of Seven Seas Fish Store grilling seafood for the employees' lunch on Good Friday, 2000.

Above: Sardines on a grill, 2000.

Right: Halder Penacho of Sea Kings Fish Store on Baldwin Street grills sardines, compliments of the house, for passersby on Good Friday, 2000.

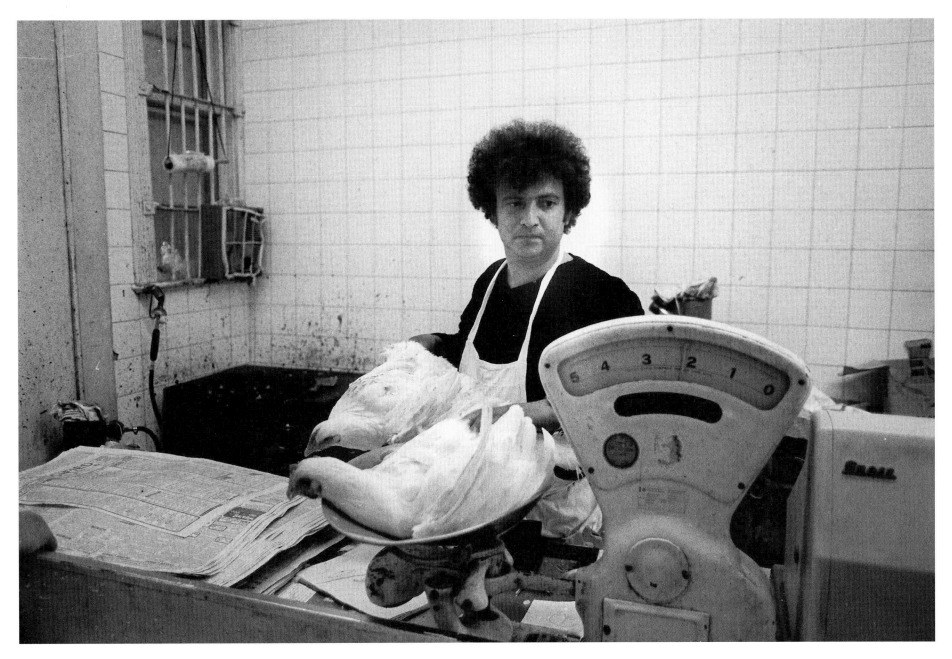

Jack Herscu, weighing live chickens for sale, Baldwin Street, 1981.

Selling pigeons on Augusta Avenue, 1981.

Left: Herman Maiato of Coral Sea Fish Store, 2000.
Right: Solly Stern, runs Max and Son Meat Market on Baldwin Street. The store was opened by his father, Max, in 1955 (2000).

Left: Christina Rossi of Casa Acoreana on a break, Augusta and Baldwin, 1999.
Right: Cafe Kim, Kensington Avenue, 2000.

A market regular relaxes in the sunshine on Baldwin Street, 2000.

A resident enjoys a quiet moment on his verandah, oblivious to the hustle and bustle of the market, Kensington Avenue, 1982.

House and stores on the corner of St. Andrew Street and Kensington Avenue, 2000.

A dramatic example of a commercial conversion that split the original gables and completely obliterated the Victorian style architecture of houses on Augusta Avenue, 1981.

A snowy day on Augusta Avenue in the 1980s.

Left: Manuel and Deolinda Moniz in their garden on Nassau Street, 1995.
Right: Pat Roy and Stewart Scriver, owners of Courage My Love, in front of their house on Kensington Avenue, 2000.

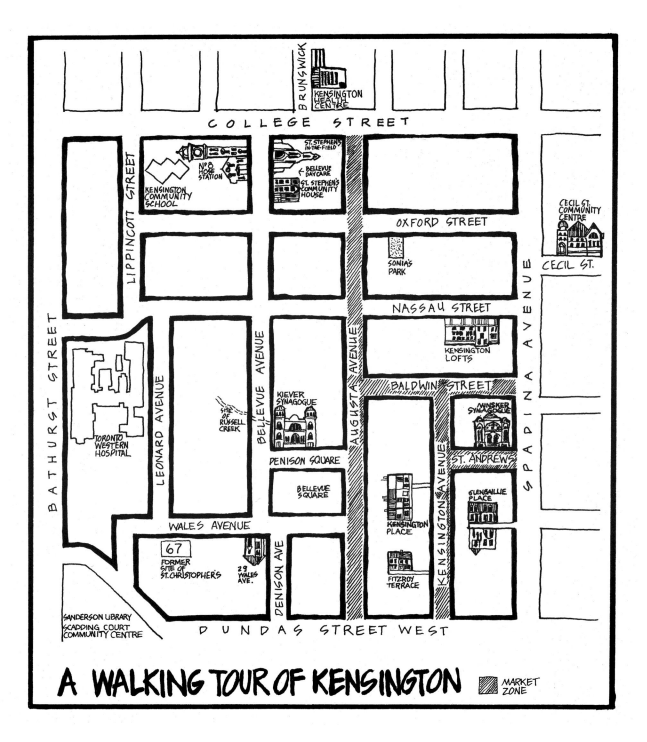

A WALKING TOUR OF KENSINGTON

MARKET ZONE

BIBLIOGRAPHY

BOOKS

Adam, G. Mercer. *Toronto Old and New: A Memorial Volume.* Toronto: The Mail Printing Co., 1891

Arthur, Eric. *Toronto, No Mean City.* Toronto: University of Toronto Press, 1964

Bayefsky, Aba. *Aba Bayefsky in Kensington Market.* Oakville: Mosaic Press, 1991

Betcherman, Lita-rose. *The Little Band: The Clashes between the Communists and the Canadian Establishment 1928–1932.* Ottawa: Deneau Publishers, 1987

Davis, Minerva. *The Wretched of the Earth and Me.* Toronto: Lugus Publications, 1992

Donegan, Rosemary, Rick Salutin, *Spadina Avenue.* Vancouver and Toronto: Douglas and McIntyre., 1985

Duff, J. Clarence with Sarah Yates. *Toronto Then & Now.* Toronto: Fitzhenry & Whiteside, 1984

Firth, Edith. *Toronto in Art, 150 Years through Artists' Eyes.* Toronto: Fitzhenry and Whiteside in co-operation with the City of Toronto, 1983

Fowler, Edmond P. *Building Cities that Work.* Montreal and Kingston: McGill-Queen's University Press, 1992

Gagan, David. *The Denison Family of Toronto, 1792–1925.* Toronto: Canadian Biographical Studies, University of Toronto Press, 1973

Gelman, Jack. *Yiddish, A Two-Way Street.* Toronto: AMA Graphics Incorporated, 1997

Harney, Robert F., ed. *Gathering Place: Peoples and Neighbourhoods of Toronto: 1834 to 1945, Studies in Ethnic and Immigration History.* Toronto: Multi-cultural History Society of Ontario, 1985

Hudson, Edna. *Bellevue Avenue: an architectural and social study.* Toronto: Toronto Region Architectural Conservancy, 1993

Irving, Allan, Harriet Parsons and Donald Bellamy. *Neighbours: Three Social Settlements in Downtown Toronto.* Toronto: Canadian Scholars' Press Inc., 1995

Kluckner, Michael. *Toronto the Way It Was.* Toronto: Whitecap Books Ltd., 1988

Lemon, James. *Toronto Since 1918, an Illustrated History, The History of Canadian Cities.* Toronto: James Lorimer & Company and National Museum of Man, National Museums of Canada, 1985

Levitt, Cyril H. and William Shaffir. *The Riot at Christie Pits.* Toronto: Lester & Orpen Dennys, 1987

Marques, Domingos and Joao Medeiros. *Portuguese Immigrants, 25 Years in Canada.* Toronto: Marquis Printers 1980

Marques, Domingos, Manuela Maruja. *With Hardened Hands—A Pictorial History of Portuguese Immigration to Canada in the 1950s.* Toronto: New Leaf Publications, 1993

Masters, D. C. *The Rise of Toronto, 1850-1890.* Toronto: University of Toronto Press, 1947

Paris, Erna, *Jews: an Account of their Experience in Canada.* Toronto: MacMillan of Canada, 1980

Rosenthal, Joe and Adele Wiseman. *Old Markets, New World.* Toronto: The MacMillan Company of Canada Limited, 1964

Speisman, Stephen A. *The Jews of Toronto: A History to 1937.* Toronto: McClelland and Stewart, 1979

MAGAZINES AND NEWSPAPERS

Bell, Margaret. "Toronto's Melting Pot." *The Canadian Magazine,* July 1913

Conologue, Ray. *The Varsity Community Issue.* University of Toronto. November 28, 1969

Fleming, James. "The Fighting Denisons." *Maclean's Magazine,* Vol XXVII, No. 2, December 1913

Leighton, Tony. "Brazen Cornucopia." *Equinox.* Toronto: November/December 1985

O'Reilly, Dan. "Council rejects appeal for live market animals." *Real Estate News.* Toronto: February 10, 1984

St. Stephen's Church Monthly and Parish Magazine. Toronto: November 1922

The Echo. Port Hope, Canada West: Church of England in Canada, January 10, 1861

The Kensington. April 1976, June 1976, January 1976

GLOBE AND MAIL

Bagnall, Kenneth. "A Hungry University." *The Globe Magazine*

Moon, Peter. "Kensington gives Moon followers a cool reception." *Globe and Mail.* August 9, 1978

"Kensington—a Supermarket with a European Accent." *Globe and Mail.* July 20, 1965

Lind, Loren. "The Kensington People Create Their Own School," *Globe and Mail.* May 11, 1971

MacIntyre, A. Lorne. "Toronto's Busiest Market on Kensington Avenue has Asiatic Atmosphere." *The Globe.* August 6, 1937

Shainbaum, Barbara. "New Faces in Kensington." *Globe and Mail.* August 30, 1980

THE KENSINGTON DRUM

McCarty, Willard. *Humanist.* December 22, 1989. *The Kensington Drum.* February/March 1990

Perlman, David. "Augusta Gas Wars Over? No, just one battle, says Gus Fisher." *The Kensington Drum.* August 31, 1989

Perlman, David. "Canopies Reprieve May Be Market Salvation." *The Kensington Drum.* August 3, 1990

Perlman, David. "Consumers Gus! Deal on gas mains in sight?" *The Kensington Drum.* November 1991

Schwam, Alan. "Twenty-two Years of Promises." *The Kensington Drum.* October/November 1989

TORONTO STAR

Allen, Glen. "Will Urban Development Kill Colourful Kensington?" *Toronto Star.* July 26, 1969

Crain, W. A. "Star Weekly Commissioner Pays a Visit to One of City's Historic Schools." *Star Weekly.* November 11, 1916

Daly, Margaret. Toronto Star. June 5, 1971

Ferri, John. "Kensington's Live Fowl Ruffle Feathers" *Toronto Star.* July 7, 1982

"New Serial: Carry On, Kensington." *Toronto Star.* March 4, 1966

Strupat, Bob. "Kensington area residents fight for the kind of school they want." *Toronto Star.* June 13, 1970

BOOKLETS

A Sense of Spadina. Canadian Jewish Congress, Central Region. Toronto: Archives, 1974

DeLaurentiis, Joanne, Lorne Brown. *Kensington Roots.* Toronto: St. Stephen's Community House, 1980

Denison, Robert Evelyn. *A History of the Denison Family in Canada, 1792–1910.* Grimsby: n.d.

Grewal, Sharanpal, Rob Kristofferson. *Voices of Justice: UNITE's History and Heritage in Canada.* Toronto: Ontario Workers Arts and Heritage Centre, 1997

Myrvold, Barbara. *Historical Walking Tour of Kensington Market and College Street.* Toronto: Toronto Public Library Board (Ontario Ministry of Culture and Communications), 1992

O'Connor, Patricia J. *The Story of St. Christopher House 1912–1984.* Toronto: The Toronto Association of Neighbourhood Services, 1986

O'Connor, Patricia J. *The Story of St. Stephen's Community House 1962–1984.* Toronto: The Toronto Association of Neighbourhood Services, 1986

Toronto Western Hospital West Winds, Volume XIII. Toronto: January 1976

REPORTS, THESES

Brown, Alderman Horace. "Miracle of Kensington, Brief for Board of Control and City Council in Relation to Kensington Area Urban Renewal Proposal." April 17, 1968

Brown, Lorne. "Market Place for a School: The story of the Kensington Community School." 1970

Bunce, Susannah C. "Sweeping the Streets: Revitalization in Kensington Market," February 1999, paper submitted to Faculty of Environmental Studies, York University

City of Toronto Planning Board. "Draft Plan for the Neighbourhood Improvement Program in Kensington." Toronto: October 1975

City of Toronto Planning Board. "Kensington Official Plan Proposals." Toronto: 1978

Clark, Chair W. H., City of Toronto Planning Board. "Report on Priorities for Urban Renewal Study Areas." Toronto: October 7, 1963

Rigby, Douglas W. "Citizen Participation in Urban Renewal Planning, A Case Study of an Inner City Residents' Association." Thesis. University of Waterloo, 1975

ARCHIVES AND LIBRARIES

Anglican Diocese of Toronto Archives

Archives of Ontario

Bell Canada Historical Services

City of Toronto Archives

Multicultural History Society of Ontario

National Archives of Canada

Ontario Jewish Archives

St. Christopher House

St. Stephen's-in-the-Field Anglican Church

St. Stephen's Community House

Sanderson Public Library

Sisterhood of St. John the Divine

Toronto District School Board Museum and Archives

Toronto Reference Library

Acknowledgments

Kensington has been a labour of love for a number of people.

When I called Heritage Toronto to discuss the Kensington book idea, Jean Cochrane's name immediately came up. She had been involved, along with her husband, Glenn Cochrane, and other volunteers, in a Heritage Toronto oral history project. They had been interviewing people in Kensington for the archives, recording the history for presentation and research purposes. Jean took to the book idea and ran with it, building on the work they had already begun. Her commitment to this project has been total. She has done it for the satisfaction of getting down on paper an accurate history of how Kensington—a community the she and Glenn are passionate about—came to be. I can't thank her enough.

Although he was juggling several other book projects at the time I approached him, photographer Vincenzo Pietropaolo agreed to get involved. Having grown up in the Italian enclave just west of Kensington, Vince clearly understands the immigrant experience in Canada. He had already photographed Kensington extensively in the early '80s, and now he has beautifully documented Kensington today. His dedication to this project has been outstanding and I am grateful for his contribution.

Our partnership with the community was key, and took the form of a resource group of former and current Kensington residents. I want to thank those people on the committee who shared their stories and photographs and helped guide us to the information. Mike Lipowski from the City of Toronto's Heritage Services Culture Division was especially helpful.

Without financial support this book would not have been possible. My sincere thanks go to the Toronto Community Foundation, the City of Toronto Millennium Fund, and Kensington Health Centre. They believed that both the process and the outcome were worth the investment.

Boston Mills Press publisher John Denison has been supportive from our first meeting. I thank him for taking on this project and providing us with a vehicle to tell the Kensington story. We appreciate his flexibility in accommodating the community process that is so vital to a project such as this. Our thanks also go to managing editor Noel Hudson, editors Kathleen Fraser and Jane Gates, and designer Mary Firth for their collaboration.

To my volunteer Board of Directors and all the staff at St. Stephen's Community House, sincere gratitude. This book is a permanent legacy to the many volunteers and staff who have made St. Stephen's such an important and recognizable part of the Kensington community and such a wonderful place to work.

And finally, I want to thank Pierre Tétrault, whom I met in the early '80s when we both lived in Kensington. He was in the process of founding KYTES—Kensington Youth Theatre Ensemble of St. Stephen's—an innovative project aimed at helping street youth get their lives back together. Along the way, while the book was unfolding, we shared many Kensington moments together. We remembered something that we both believe in—that with creativity and compassion you can build caring, healthy communities.

Liane Regendanz
Executive Director
St. Stephen's Community House
June 2000

The following are offered special thanks for their assistance, their memories, their knowledge and their photographs.

Archie Alleyne
Fatima Alves
Hy Beck
Frances Borg
Lorne Brown
Ida Carnevali
Kirk Cheney
Glenn Cochrane
Ron Daiter
Maria Da Silva
Nick Da Silva
Harry David
Brenda Duncombe
Bob Ellis
Maureen Fair
Susan Fagen
Peter Firkola
Gus Fisher
The Rev. Kevin Flynn
Jack Gelman
Isabel Gomes
Tam Goossen
Desi Gouveia

Maria Gouveia
Yvonne Grant
Dr. Cyril Greenland
Harry Greenspan
Martin Gries
Morris Grossberger
Rose Grossberger
Joanne Harburn
Keith Harburn
Alice Heap
The Rev. Dan Heap
Heritage Toronto, Heritage Services, Culture Division, City of Toronto
Steve Johnston
Marion Kane
Max Katz
Sadie Katz
Kensington Market Action Committee
Sam Krakowski
Wendy Kwong
Ray Landry
Mel Lastman
Al Liebowitz
Mike Lipowski

Sam Lunansky
Peter Matyas
Morris Miller
Don McKellar
George McKenna
David Melville
Tom Mihalik
Tammy O'Dwyer
Joe Oksenhendler
Sid Palmer
Captain Donald Paterson
Victor Pavao
David Perlman
Mary Perlmutar
Morris Perlmutar
David Pinkus
Vanessa Porteous
Liane Regendanz
Joe Rosenthal
Honey Ross
Oscar Ross
Pat Roy
The Rev. Campbell Russell
Maria Santos
Christina Chu Schwam
Ava Schwevell
Kate Scowen
Stewart Scriver

Carol Slavic
Brian Smith
Al Soren
Stephen Speisman
Solly Stern
Percy Stone
Jenny Tomaz
Jose Tomaz
Mary Betty Tomaz
Channah Van Graft
Arnold Weinberg
Arnold Winn
Beryl Yates
Danny Zimmerman
Molly Zimmerman

☆

Thanks also go to donors who helped to make the publication of this book possible:

The Toronto Community Foundation

The City of Toronto Millennium Fund

Kensington Health Centre